Storytelling

3 Manuscripts in 1 Book, Including: How to Tell a Story, How to Write Fiction and How to Write Content

Jaiden Pemton

More by Jaiden Pemton

Discover all books from the Creative Writing Series by Jaiden Pemton at:

bit.ly/jaiden-pemton

Book 1: *How to Write Fiction*

Book 2: *How to Tell a Story*

Book 3: *How to Write a Screenplay*

Book 4: *How to Write Sales Copy*

Book 5: *How to Edit Writing*

Book 6: *How to Self-Publish*

Book 7: *How to Write Non-Fiction*

Book 8: *How to Write Content*

Themed book bundles available at discounted prices:

bit.ly/jaiden-pemton

Copyright

Under no circumstances will any legal responsibility or blame be held against the publisher for any reparation, damages, or monetary loss due to the information herein, either directly or indirectly.

Respective authors own all copyrights not held by the publisher.

The information herein is offered for informational purposes solely, and is universal as so. The presentation of the information is without contract or any type of guarantee assurance.

The trademarks that are used are without any consent, and the publication of the trademark is without permission or backing by the trademark owner. All trademarks and brands within this book are for clarifying purposes only and are the owned by the owners themselves, not affiliated with this document.

Table of Contents

Book 1: How to Tell a Story

7 Easy Steps to Master Storytelling, Story Boarding, Writing Stories, Storyteller & Story Structure

Jaiden Pemton

Introduction

There is a magic in storytelling that has been present and passed down from generation to generation. When you tell a story, you have the entire world at your fingertips, and you can relay the message to your audience in any way you desire. Storytelling gives you the power to create life-altering emotional experiences for the people reading and listening, and it provides your personal experiences. It values the ability to live on forever.

When it comes to storytelling, it can be easy to get carried away and find your audience feeling lost or not being able to understand the point of the story. It is easy to fall into the trap of including too many details, or not enough, in speaking too long, using the unappealing language for your audience, or creating an emotionally flat story. There are several elements to keep in mind to ensure that your audience is engaged and that your story will live on with them, and be passed on to others for years to come.

Storytelling can seem like a daunting task, especially in today's age, where people have short attention spans and difficulty creating emotional connections to the stories being told to them. That said, there is still hope for storytellers to engage people with what they are saying and for their message to have the desired impact. All it takes is an in-depth knowledge of the storytelling elements that will make your readers and listeners care about what is being told to them and want to stick around for the shining moment.

This guide will serve as your step-by step reference through the realm of storytelling — breaking down the details within each step of the process and helping you to understand what makes your stories essential and how to relay that to your audience.

The chapters of this guide will take you through each step of storytelling in a way that will help you check all the boxes and avoid common mistakes. Together, we will explore the best techniques for developing your plot, knowing your audience, keeping audience engagement levels high, creating an emotional experience for your audience, tying your narrative in to increase levels of empathy, maintaining an element of surprise, and establishing a shining moment which can maintain the test of time. Each detail is designed to keep you on track and answer any questions you may have about the storytelling process. Throughout the journey, you will find yourself discovering the importance of the life experiences you have had that have led you to the point of wanting to tell this story and how you can use your life experience to change your audience's lives.

Each chapter is organized in an easy-to-follow, subtitled format with comprehensive examples of every tip, trick, and technique. This all-inclusive guide to storytelling also contains a few exclusive secrets and information that can help you further develop your skills and create impactful stories.

Whether you are aiming to tell stories directly as they happened in your life, with yourself as the central character, or stories which are loosely based on your experience but center around other characters and a fantasy plot, this guide has all the tools you need and is sure to serve as the perfect guide to revolutionize your storytelling experience.

Happy writing!

Chapter 1: Step 1 - Establishing Purpose and Structure

When it comes to storytelling, it is vital to know the reason you have to tell the story. What makes it essential; what message needs to be relayed to the world through your story? How will this story be unlike anything else, and how will its message speak for itself and stick with the audience?

Defining the Take-Away

Any successful story must begin with a takeaway message. Think back to the stories you have heard in the past that you think of often. Perhaps these are stories that you find yourself re-telling to other people, or always find yourself asking to hear or read again. These are the stories that shape how you approach your daily life—the stories you can never tire of hearing.

To tell a powerful story, you must deliver a message that will have the same long-lasting impact on your audience. You should strive for the stories you tell to be those your audience will apply to their life over and over again. Imagine, for example, your grandfather telling you a story about the bracelet he never takes off, which was given to him by a friend and fellow soldier in World War II. In this story, your grandfather defines the power of friendship as he narrates how he and this man became friends. He includes the conflict and challenges they overcame throughout the war and describes the particular battle in which his friend was shot. With tears in his eyes, he describes the way he felt his heartbreak on the battlefield as his best friend died in his arms. This story's takeaway is the power of friendship and how it persists through challenges and even through a great loss.

Keeping the Story on Track

The message of your story should be present from the beginning and become stronger as the story unfolds. Everything that happens throughout the story should build-up to the end, which is the most important part. You should describe in only a sentence or two what your audience should take away from the story, and build up to that as you craft the story. It is your job as the storyteller to guide your listeners/readers by unfolding the story to ensure that the message has an intended impact. Before beginning, you must have an understanding of what tone your message carries. Is this a funny story? A reality check? Is it intended to inspire the audience to be better people? Is it a vulnerable, emotional story that will make the audience think differently about something? It is your job to keep the tone of your message alive as you guide your readers/listeners through the story.

In the story of the grandfather who lost his best friend in World War II, for example, the importance of friendship is evident from the beginning. As your grandfather describes the experiences he had with his friend, both positive and negative, and their day-to-day life in the war, the theme of friendship prevails. You see both their happiest memories and the most significant challenges and the importance of their friendship in keeping each other going through the hardest times. The heart-shattering image of his friend being killed in battle and dying in his arms drives in the power of friendship, even in the moments of the most bitter loss. From here, it is clear to see how the power of friendship lives on, no matter what.

Defining your Goals

If the story is meant to be a reality check, you will want to provide your audience with an "I used to think this, but now I think this," moment. If your goal is to be funny, you'll need to ensure you have humor stitched throughout the plot, and you'll want to make sure the twist in the story is one that will make your audience laugh harder than they have in years. If the story is about morals, you will need to incorporate examples that cause the audience to think about moral decisions from a variety of perspectives and develop a strong sense of right and wrong within the context of the story. Keeping your listeners/readers engaged requires the use of dramatic tension and suspense to keep your audience on the edge of their seats, hardly able to stand the anticipation at what will happen next. No matter which direction you take with your story, you must clearly define the central theme.

Structure: Mapping it Out

When thinking about how to story structure, you should imagine your main message as the destination and the unfolding of the story as the destination. Each component of the structure can serve as a marker on the map to where you want your audience to end up. There are three large markers on the storytelling map: the inciting incident, rising action, climax, and resolution. Your navigation tools are 2 C's: Characters and conflict. These are the things that will keep your audience moving on their journey.

The starting place of your map is the character introduction and initial conflict. Regardless of who your characters are, you will need to introduce them quickly. Ensure the audience understands who each character is and what they mean to the story as you move into the actions. If you are the main character in your story, ensure that it is clear from the very beginning. It is important to provide great detail in your character descriptions.

Suppose the characters in your story have defining characteristics or elements of physical appearance, for example. In that case, a particular tattoo, style of dress, voice, or talent, this should be clear from the beginning. Establishing your characters in this way and building upon what makes them stand out will allow your audience to establish an immediate connection. To avoid overwhelming your audience and causing them to confuse characters, try to keep the number of characters in the story low.

If you are telling a personal story, there will likely only be a few central characters. If you are writing a story that is not based upon an event in your personal life, make sure you don't get carried away in the character planning. Try to stick to between three and five characters, and ensure that there is one central character.

Exploring the 2 C's: Character and Conflict

Your story's central character (whether it is yourself or someone else) should very quickly come into conflict with a force that challenges their character. Let's say, for example, that the character in your story is an exchange student traveling to a foreign country.

From the very beginning, you will want to clarify details about this person, such as where they come from, where they are going, and why. Perhaps they just graduated high school and felt the need to explore something new before starting college. The message of a story like this may be learning that love can overcome all boundaries and that the relationships people share are the most crucial thing with life. In this instance, let's imagine the story opens by putting the reader/listener in a moment with the exchange student on the plane, thinking about everything they are about to undertake. An example of an initial conflict that is on track with the story's message is the exchange student getting lost in an airport where hardly anyone speaks their language and begins to feel less confident and capable about their journey.

As the student attempts to navigate the airport, perhaps they also lose one of their bags or miss their flight. The student is likely feeling exhausted, defeated, and unsure of themselves and their journey. Be sure that as you introduce your characters and initial challenge, that you play into describing the surroundings. What time in history is it? What time of day? How can you describe the place this person is in and what emotions that setting invokes on them? Are they with other people or alone? The tension of this initial challenge is what will move the story forward towards the climax.

After this initial conflict, the rest of the story will likely deal with how the exchange student humbles themselves, learns the language of the country they are going to, and comes to understand the power of human interaction and relationships beyond language.

During this initial challenge to the main character, you should focus on inflicting tension and a sense of conflict that makes the reader think, connect, and wonder what will happen next. In the case of the exchange student story, imagine the story beginning, and ending, in the same airport, but with entirely different outcomes after the student has spent a year living abroad. If you are writing a funny story, consider building the humor up slowly, with small details that will make the final punchline all the more memorable.

Tying it All Together

Resolution is the next step after the climax has occurred. This is the part of the story that allows your audience to wind down and settle into the story's deeper meaning. This should be something that satisfies them and brings all of the story's other events full circle. In the case of the story with the exchange student, for example, we might see a resolution in which they are in the same airport they once got lost in, interacting freely with those around them and breathing in their last moments in that country, thinking of all their memories and how far they have come. These memories can serve as a callback to events that happened in earlier parts of the story and truly frame the audience's takeaway message.

Even in stories with a sad ending, such as the story of the grandfather's friendship with a fellow soldier killed in World War II, the audience will feel satisfied and inspired by the depth and power of friendship. Their hearts will be moved by the high emotionality of the story and the way that even though your grandfather's friend died much too soon, the power of their friendship could never die.

Assuming the Role of a Screenwriter

An excellent way to think about the structure of your story is to envision it as a movie. Imagine one of your favorite movies and how it unfolds to arrive at the screenwriter's message. Put yourself in the screenwriter's role and imagine a beginning, middle, and end of the story that will leave your reader feeling impacted and satisfied. It is crucial to carefully consider each of your story parts to avoid your audience becoming bored from the beginning, lost in the middle, or feeling completely dissatisfied at the end.

Chapter 2: Step 2 - Bringing the Audience In

The most compelling element of a good storyteller is the ability to keep the audience engaged from start to finish. To keep an audience engaged, you must first understand your audience. Different styles, lengths of stories, and messages will appeal to and be received by different groups. The story needs to be relevant to your audience. It is your job as the designer of the story to find points of interest that are specifically catered to your audience context and demographic. Whether your story is being presented to a classroom of Millennials, a business workplace, a group of elementary school-aged children, a group of Baby Boomers, or a particular religious group, you need to understand which styles of storytelling appeal to each of these groups, as well as what sort of attention span you can expect.

The tone to take with each of these groups varies greatly, and you can completely determine the impact of your story based upon how professional, friendly, vulnerable, approachable, fantastical, or down-to-earth your audience expects you to be.

Knowing your Audience

Your audience's understanding should determine which language you use to tell your story, which details will be most important to that audience, and how long you will take to write/tell the story. It is important never to assume that the audience knows everything you do. You need to do everything you can to avoid specialized language that will make people feel like outsiders and lose connection. This can include the use of abstract concepts or names that could cause more confusion than clarification from your audience.

In a dynamic, fast-paced workplace environment, or to a classroom of young people with short attention spans, you will not want your story to take longer than a few minutes to listen to or read through. At a specialized conference, however, your audience may be able to maintain engagement with a longer story. That being said, any story that drags on and on will eventually cause people's attention to wane. Some of the most meaningful stories are those which can unfold in a few words. Keep this in mind and try to make the story only as long as it needs to be to come full circle and leave the audience feeling satisfied.

Bridging the Gap

Once you have determined who your audience is, you must seek out where you can build a bridge between your characters and yourself. This story is yours, and you must establish a relationship between yourself and the audience.

Suppose you are speaking to an audience of college students, forever. In that case, you may establish a sense of relatability and "bridge the gap" by sharing a relevant story from when you were in college yourself. It is important to consider your relationship with the audience and what will make them feel connected to you and the story you have to share.

The bridge between your audience and your story goes two ways. To be fair to the audience, you must question your motivations in writing the story, and ensure that you will be able to approach it in a way that both speaks your message and keeps your listeners feeling connected.

Methods for Capturing Audience Attention

It is crucial to capture your audience's attention from the beginning of the story. One way to do this is by showing yourself or your main character (if it is not yourself) as someone likable. This can be established through humor or discussing a certain personal value.

Another way to establish audience engagement is by providing a point of connection between them and yourself or your main character through vulnerability. Sharing something personal and authentic is a great way to make your audience settle into the story and become invested in how things play out. There are comfort and appreciation provided by the vulnerability, and it has the power to set the tone for the rest of the story.

A final approach you may take in initial audience engagement is piquing their curiosity with a question, or by dropping them into an intense moment with little context. As your story unfolds, your mission is either to answer the question you posed, or provide context to the moment you described at the beginning. Suppose you begin your story with a question. In that case, you will ultimately be erasing any boundaries between your audience and your stories by making the audience feel that they are a central part of the story. If they feel that the narrative is unfolding around them, not outside of them, they are much more likely to stay engaged until the end and experience the unfolding of the story in a real, personal way.

Making your Audience Care

Regardless of which approach you to take; it is crucial to make your audience care. If the story starts too slow or begins to fall off track in the middle, your audience will lose interest and decide that they no longer care about what will happen next. This is especially true for people in today's fast-paced society. We live among people who gloss over texts and half-listen to others while thinking more about what they will say or do next. If it is not clear to you how your story is meaningful to a particular audience, it will certainly not be clear to the audience. To keep your audience presence throughout your story, they have to feel invested in the experience and see it as something that will benefit them somehow.

The WIIFM test stands for "What's in it for me." This is something your audience automatically wants to know. How can your story apply to their life? Will it inspire them? Open their mind? Teach them a new skill to make use of? Make them laugh, cry, or develop frustration which can fuel action?

Using the Power of Language

Another element of audience engagement is the use of vivid language and intonation. The power of language is universal, and you can use the tools of idiom, parables, and metaphors to inflict an emotional response from your audience. In the Biblical *parable of the Good Shepherd,* Jesus' love of his flock is symbolic of love for humanity as a whole. When one sheep wanders away from the flock, Jesus pursues that sheep until it has returned. The power of calling each sheep by name creates a feeling of personal connection and importance to the audience members.

Appealing to Audience Needs

When it comes to the art of storytelling, the audience's needs must be at the focus. This is a universal truth that surpasses cultural and traditional boundaries and contexts. Stories change slightly depending upon who it is being told to and where they're coming from. Good storytellers can meet their readers/listeners where they're at and focus upon what they seek and what will inspire them in the future.

Chapter 3: Step 3 - Making it Personal

A personal narrative is one of the most powerful tools you have at your disposal in the art of storytelling. This can take the form of telling a story that centers around you as the main character and an event that has occurred in your life. However, a personal narrative can also be infused into characters and scenarios you create. You can develop a mostly fictional story but maintains elements of your personal experience to keep the level of relatability alive. If there is one thing everyone can relate to, it is that we are all human beings with stories. It is vital to use elements of your own life to make waves in the art of storytelling.

If you choose not to tell your story from direct personal experience, the inspiration you draw from scenarios in your life can bring stories to life. Not only can this be a source of liberation in the way it allows you to bring elements of your experience to life in the way you see fit, but it is also crucial to storyteller/audience relations as well. In the example of the story of the friends from World War II, if you were choosing to write this story about your grandfather's experience, you would need to build that connection with him on a human level and determine how to relay that connection to your audience.

Making it Relatable

One of the most important things about sharing the personal narrative is the way it enhances the relatability factor between the storyteller and the audience. If your personal experience is tied into your story, the audience will be inspired to gain a deeper understanding of ultimately grows in empathy. The more people can empathize with the characters of a particular story, the more of an impact that story will have.

Let's consider you are telling a story to a class of college students regarding your own experiences in college. The goal of the story is to make them care about managing their time in college. A good way to keep them engaged is to start with a narrative they can relate to. For example, imagine you spent the night off campus one day and woke up late on the day of your first college exam. Not only are you late, but you also don't have the time to study for your exam that you had planned to take by waking up three hours beforehand to study. In the story, you leap from your bed frantically, throw on your clothes, and attempt to mumble what you could remember from your notes as you dashed out the door to your car.

On the way, you spill coffee all over your shirt. You are driving down the road, not paying attention, trying desperately to recall enough information to pass your first exam, when all of a sudden, you hear a horrible scraping noise on the side of your car. You look and see that you have hit one of the cars parked on the side of the street and that both of your mirrors have fallen off. At this point, you are twenty minutes late for your exam and have to email your professor and ask to go to his office to take it later. The message of this story is the importance of getting enough sleep and studying ahead of time, as well as not making decisions such as sleeping off campus the night before a big exam. By presenting an event that students can probably relate to some degree, your message will clearly come across.

Maintaining Balance of Details

An important thing to keep in mind if you are telling a true story is not to get carried away with details. If you include every single detail of the experience, it is much more likely that your audience will become lost and have difficulty distinguishing what is happening. This is another place where you must be critical and think about what your audience needs. Ask yourself which details are most crucial to the message of the story and which elements will be most likely to stick with your audience.

After determining the beginning and end of your story, dedicate your attention to the middle's details. Ensure that you provide enough detail to set the scene, but not so much that the message becomes muddled.

Writers Tip: Create a bulleted list of points in the plots which will occur between the beginning and end of your story. Check over the list several times, keeping in mind your message and the needs of the audience. Don't hesitate to add or take points off as needed.

Chapter 4: Step 4 - Creating an Emotional Experience

Think back to the last book you read, or film you watched, that seemed to take you beyond this realm of time and space and commanded your focus completely. If it was a book, perhaps it was one that you could not put down until the end, and if it was a movie, perhaps it was one that took you to an alternative reality and kept you on the edge of your seat with intensity. When it comes to your storytelling endeavors, you should strive to inflict these same feelings on your audience. This requires a great deal of attention to detail to ensure you create an atmosphere of intensity that will keep your audience emotionally involved. It is important to consider ahead of time which emotions you wish to play into. Should this story make your audience feel joyful? Inspired? Light-hearted? Melancholic?

Angry? Suspenseful? Take some time before you begin your story to narrow down the emotional experience you want the audience to have.

Setting the Scene

To capture your audience's senses and create an emotional experience, it is necessary to set a scene. Where is this story unfolding? What does the air smell like? What are the sights and sounds of the area? Keep in mind the time of year and the geographical location, as both of these things will inflict some sort of emotional response in your audience. If your audience feels immersed in the experience of a sea-side village, for example, they will be more likely to connect with the events that transpire there.

Embracing Conflict

It is crucial to embrace conflict as a storyteller—the conflict of the story is what will invoke the most emotions in your audience and keep them most heavily engaged. As you are crafting your narrative, consider each scene in depth. What obstacle does your main character (or yourself) face in each scene, and how do they overcome them? How should this obstacle make the audience feel? To achieve audience satisfaction when you reach the end of the story, you must cause them to experience the struggles of the main characters as they work to achieve their goals.

Examples of the Emotional Experience Scene 1

Let's go back to the story of the exchange student. In Scene 1, the audience is introduced to the character of the exchange student. They learn that she is from a small town in rural Nebraska, where she has lived for the entire eighteen years of her life. She is surrounded by people doing all the same things: graduating from high school, going to college or adopting a trade in the state, getting married, having kids, and staying in Nebraska until they die. She has always had a deep desire to see what the world has to offer outside of her small town, and she was thrilled when she stumbled across the opportunity to apply to be an exchange student. Now, she is finally on her way and is full of nervous excitement for all the unpredictability that she knows awaits her. This first scene invokes the emotion of excitement within your readers.

Examples of the Emotional Experience Scene 2

Now, let's move to Scene 2 of this story. In Scene 2, the exchange student has had two connecting flights and has landed at the airport of Sao Paulo, Brazil. This is her last stop before getting on her final flight to the city she will be staying in. Upon landing, she is unable to find her bags at the designated pick-up area and must embark on a nerve-wracking journey around the airport to find them. Because she can hardly speak Portuguese, and cannot find any attendants who speak English, she is faced with having to type phrases into Google Translate, holding them up to every attendant she sees and hoping they will be able to help her.

Meanwhile, she has no idea how to get to her next gate and has less than an hour before her flight will be taking off. As she runs around frantically, sleep-deprived, unable to communicate with those around her, and completely alone, the audience will have the same kind of tense, anxiety-ridden emotional experience that she is having. As the conflict mounts, the audience will be on the edge of their seats wondering if she will find her bags and get on the right flight, or if she will end up stuck in the airport trying to figure out what to do next.

Examples of the Emotional Experience Scene 3

In Scene 3, she stumbles upon her bags, which is a relief. However, after re-checking her bags, she has twenty minutes to get to her gate and no idea how to get there. She is going up and down escalators, running this way and that down the corridor, trying the same methods to speak with attendants, and nothing is working. Eventually, just as she has resigned herself to the reality that she will miss her flight, a young man about her age emerges from nowhere and comes up to her. He speaks in English, asking her "Are you lost?"

She learns that this boy is returning from a several weeks stay in New York, before which he was doing an exchange year in Ireland. He tells her he knew she was an exchange student because of her blazer and her lost expression. Shockingly, he reveals to her that they are going to the same city in Brazil and leads her to the correct gate. Before they board the plane, he gives her his phone number to reach out if she needs anything upon arrival. This young man becomes her best friend, and the core of her friend group in Brazil—he is the first person she meets within the circle of people who show her what love is, and how it can surpass all barriers. Of course, this moment fills the audience with emotions of relief and surprise at the irony of events.

Examples of the Emotional Experience Scene 4

In Scene 4, let's imagine the exchange student is back in the same airport one year later, after learning the Portuguese language and developing the closest relationships of her life with the young man she met at the airport, two other Brazilian women, and six exchange students from around the world who all lived in the same city. As she looks around at the surroundings, all the same as the last day she was there, and finds herself easily able to read the signs and converse with the attendants, she begins to cry tears of nostalgia and gratitude. She thinks to herself how this experience has been more than she ever could have asked for, and her heart feels broken in the best way possible from the kind of love she came to know while overseas. At this moment, the reader will feel satisfied as everything has come full circle and the student has reached her goals of finding a home in this foreign place. They will feel her pain in missing the people in whom she built her home, and their hearts will be full of the love she has come to know.

Bringing Joy to Yourself and the Audience

One of the most extraordinary things about storytelling about an experience that has meaning to you (whether it happened to you personally or not) is the joy it can bring to the storyteller. Through the art of storytelling, you can channel your personal emotional experience, adventures, and a message that is important to you, into a medium where they can live on forever. Perhaps the thing that makes storytelling most profound is how stories can be passed on from person to person, like gifts, and they bring joy to everyone who reads them. Stories have the power to light people's way into the future, and good stories never die.

Chapter 5: Step 5 - Writing the Unexpected

As human beings, we are full of stories. It is reasonable to claim that our lives are formed by the stories we hear (and remember) from others and the experiences we live, which become our own stories. Considering that we are flooded with thousands of stories throughout existence, it takes special work to make yours stand out. What will you do so that your readers will not only be impacted by your story but also will carry that impact with them into the rest of their lives?

Defying the Odds

To pull this off, you must be able to defy norms and go against the reader/listener's expectations to keep them engaged. Any element that works against your character's central desire is great to keep the reader engaged and keep the story moving forward. If you want your story to be one-of-a-kind, you have to write the unexpected. From the beginning of your story to the end, the audience should be faced with moment after moment that surprises them, makes them think differently, and overall keeps them in a state of awe. You may choose to take unusual directions in dialogue, setting, and characterization, and the best storytellers know how to use these things to give the story a memorable twist.

Developing your "Hook"

From the moment you begin your story, you have to be able to hook your reader. If you don't open the story in a way that strikes them, they will quickly lose interest and may stop paying attention.

There is no time in storytelling to "wait for it to get good"—it needs to be good from the start. It is essential to include an explosive moment in the introduction, which will grip your reader's heart, stir their emotions, and captivate their attention. Let's say, for example, you are writing a story that begins with a woman riding the bus into the city. From the beginning, you want to establish why she is riding the bus— perhaps she was recently in a car accident and has no vehicle.

You could begin the story by vaguely describing the setting, where she is going, and why she is on the bus. However, this narrative can become a lot more interesting and hook the audience if the story begins with a brief description of the setting, then the woman leans her head on her hand, closes her eyes, and begins to have flashbacks to a seizure she had while driving, which caused her car accident and thus, caused her to start taking the bus. This unexpected moment of the car accident flashback is much more intense. It gives the reader extra insight into the woman's life and a struggle she has already faced, which is more likely to keep the audience's attention.

Thinking Outside the Box with Conflict: Context, Flashback, Goals

When it comes to conflict, it would be easy to develop something like the woman getting caught in the rain or missing her bus. The problem with these conflicts is that they are to be expected when it comes to buses. To write the unexpected with your conflict, try to think outside the box. What other battles could this woman be facing?

Perhaps she takes the same bus every day to her job, and notices the same man on the bus almost every day, scribbling in his notebook. She is fascinated by how he appears and the energy he gives off, and she wants to talk to him. However, her mystery medical condition and potential for seizures drive her away from speaking to him, and she is too anxious to approach him. At this point, it is vital to provide some background information for context about her mystery illness, her uncertainty for her future, and perhaps how her illness impacted her last romantic relationship. This utilizes the flashback tool, which can provide the reader with more information and understanding of the depth of this character.

You could continue to write the unexpected by describing the complications the woman faces every day with her medical conditions, in more settings than simply on the bus. You could describe her lonely nights at home where she lives with her sister who is caring for her, her anxiety-ridden days at work, and endless trips to the hospital with no answers. Every day, the man on the bus is her ray of light, but she continues not to speak to him. At this point, talking to the man is her primary goal, with an overall goal of overcoming her fears, understanding her illness, and ultimately being able to love again.

Element of Surprise in the Climax

Now, let's imagine a scene where the man breaks the daily trend and asks if he can sit by her one morning on the bus. She obliges, they begin to talk, and then he invites her to coffee. They begin to form a relationship, but she keeps her guard up because she does not want to reveal her illness's secrets.

She tries to keep their interactions short, keep her sister on call, and enters every date with a silent prayer that she will not have a medical episode. This goes on until one night while they are having dinner at his apartment, she has a massive seizure and has to be taken to the hospital. This is the climax of the story, as her main goals come into question and her secret comes out.

Element of Surprise in the Falling Action and Resolution

To write the unexpected for this story's falling action, consider that the woman wakes up in the hospital to both her sister and the man beside her hospital bed. She breaks down and tells the man everything about her past, and how she does not know how anyone could love her under her condition, especially since there are so many unknowns. The man then reveals that he has such crippling social anxiety, he never believed he could approach a woman and talk to her, let alone find love. He admits to her that he is a poet and that every day they rode the bus together until he spoke to her, he had been writing poems for her. He had created a series in his journal called "The Woman on the Bus", in which he wrote down all the things he wished he could say to her but lacked the courage to. The man tells her that she has been his light, has given him space where he feels seen, and that he wants her no matter what. They both have health issues that seem invisible but impact them on a deep level, and they have found each other to work through those issues with. Once the woman gets out of the hospital, they continue together, loving each other and living their best lives. They both dedicate their time to creative ways to make people with disabilities, whether mental or physical, visible or invisible, feel seen, and deserving of love. This is an example of writing the unexpected in the resolution, as it takes the reader on a wild ride from hearing about a car accident and a mystery illness, to the conflict of falling in love and being too afraid to speak on it, to another conflict of keeping secrets as a romantic relationship deepens, to a scary medical incident, to a secret revealed about the other character, and finally, to an unexpected theme of love and the complexities of disability.

Brainstorming a Surprising Plot

If you are struggling to determine an adequately exciting plot, give yourself some time to brainstorm. Think of all of the sorts of things that could happen to your protagonist, and write them down. These events may be related to each other, but they do not have to be.

In this case, there were several exciting elements to the story.

1. The woman was struggling to be where she wanted to be in life

2. Had almost lost her life in a car accident

3. Had severe medical issues that no doctor could figure out

4. Had a tragic love story from her past relationship

5. Felt like her medical issues kept her from having the life she wanted

6. Fell in love with a man on the bus that she was too afraid to talk to

7. Eventually, he approached her

8. The two fell in love, but she was terrified to get too close

9. She ended up having a medical emergency and he figured out her secrets

10. He admits to her that he also has secrets regarding mental health issues that also make it hard for him to be where he wants in life

11. They end up pursuing a relationship together and changing the community by providing services to those with physical and mental illnesses/disabilities

Types of Conflict

Considering that conflict is one of the most critical elements of storytelling, it deserves a lot of attention when it comes to the prospect of writing the unexpected. As previously mentioned, conflict is the opposition that occurs between the character(s) and an internal or external force. Several ideas for potential disputes are as follows:

-Protagonist against nature: in which the protagonist faces challenges that arise from natural causes

-Protagonist against self: in which the protagonist is their most significant barrier to getting what they want, and they stand in their own way as a result of personal struggles and shortcomings.

-Protagonist against God: protagonist struggles against a sovereign force much greater than themselves, and their struggles seem practically inevitable and unavoidable.

-Protagonist against another individual: another character in the story does something that prohibits the protagonist from meeting their goal, and the protagonist must find a way to overcome it.

-Protagonist against society: the protagonist sees things differently or has different goals than the people around them, and no one seems to be on their side.

In the story idea, we see examples of the Protagonist against self as both characters battle with themselves on the journey of love.

Use of Progression

No matter what your conflict is, there are several things you need to keep in mind to keep your reader engaged and truly write something unexpected and memorable.

The first element of conflict to keep in mind is progression. Throughout the story, the protagonist's number and type of obstacles should be increasing and intensifying. In the story example, we see how the conflict goes from having to take the bus and being without a car, to having traumatic flashbacks, to living a life of doctor's appointments without answers and a life without direction, to the fear of love, to a medical emergency, and then to a plot twist moment of truth. This is an example of the progression of conflict in writing the unexpected.

Use of Mystery

Another critical aspect of the conflict is a mystery. It is essential to only explain things enough to give readers an idea, while still managing to keep them on the edge of their seats throughout the conflict. It is vital to avoid giving anything away before it is time. Along with that, it is crucial to maintain an element of surprise.

Keep things complex, engaging, and ready to go in any direction to keep the reader from being able to predict what happens next. By maintaining mystery and surprise elements, you are going against the audience's expectations and leaving them feeling more heavily impacted by what happened in the story.

Use of Empathy

Empathy also matters in writing the unexpected through conflict because it creates relationships between the characters and the audience. Often, the reader may be surprised by their connection with certain characters. They may find themselves rooting for someone they didn't expect to root for, or identifying with something they would never have imagined identifying with before. By creating this sense of empathy, the audience will find the characters' experiences resonating with them, whether in pleasant or unpleasant ways.

Use of Insight and Universality

Insight and universality are two other essential elements. The story should reveal something about human nature. In this story, there are several aspects of human nature revealed. The first is the idea surrounding struggle, and not being where you want to be in life.

The second is the deep and often terrifying experience of falling in love and letting another person see all of who you are. However, at the end of the day, this story demonstrates that the power of love, honesty, and compassion is more significant than any obstacle. In terms of universality, this story presents struggles that most readers, from most cultures, backgrounds, etc. will resonate with, simply because they are human. No matter where you are, what beliefs you hold, or what your personal experience has been, everyone can understand the power and complication of love, how it feels to be afraid, and what it is like to be kicked by life when you're down. People will care about this story because they care about love, about facing fears, and about being able to find purpose in life.

Creating a High Stakes Environment

Lastly, it is vital to create a high stakes environment surrounding the story's conflict. To keep the audience engaged, they must know that the story matters. There has to be something at stake—something precious that could be lost. To write the unexpected, consider what is at stake and the unique difficulties that pose a threat to that thing.

Experimenting with Point of View

One tip to apply to the process of writing the unexpected is to experiment with a variety of points of view. You can maintain an element of surprise and interest by writing the story in a unique style or from a voice the audience wouldn't expect. Once you have written your story, try out the effects of various points of view. Just remember, do not give the narration to a nonessential character. The storyline must revolve around a character who is central to the action, to avoid audience confusion.

Chapter 6: Step 6 - Build up to a Positive Outcome

The most important part of storytelling is the feelings you invoke in your audience at the end. As a storyteller, it is your job to bring things full circle and make it clear to the audience why everything happened the way it did and the more profound message of the story. If you leave the audience hanging and unable to identify the point, they will feel a sense of dissatisfaction with the story as a whole. One crucial part of the storytelling process is building up the sequence of events to a positive outcome.

Bringing the Story Full Circle

In both of the story ideas we discussed previously in this guide, we saw how the events the characters experienced led them to a happy and satisfying ending. The exchange student endured the difficulties of doubting her decisions and feeling lost and alone. Still, over time her experience built her into someone who not only had new language skills and cultural understanding but also an understanding of humanity itself on a deeper level and the strength of connections among humans.

In the woman's story on the bus, several things are happening that make her life extremely difficult. The reader may be left to wonder if she will ever find love or fulfillment, or if she will even be able to survive for long with her invisible medical condition. Will she ever get a diagnosis? Will this illness end up claiming her life entirely? At the end of the story, there is a resolution in the case of the woman finding love and the connection she makes with another person who has struggled with succeeding in society and feeling deserving of love. Although it is not clear if the woman will live a long life, the audience is provided with the positive outcome of the relationship between the man and the woman, the life they begin to build together, and how they help other people based upon their experiences.

Tying Positive Outcome to Emotional Experience

Although both of these stories have relatively "happy endings", a positive outcome does not always have to be happy. Consider, for example, the last time someone told you about an incredibly sad film, but also exceptionally good. Some of the best stories have endings in which somebody dies, the couple doesn't end up together, etc. but if these stories are told right, they speak to live and create a deeper sense of awareness within the audience. These endings can be even better than "happy endings", because life is a never-ending cycle of conflict, resolution, and learning experiences, and "happy endings" do not truly exist on a human level. The ending can make the reader feel sad, angry, or solemn, and individual audience members may even decide that they hate the story. However, as long as there is a profound emotional impact, and the audience can somewhat understand why things happened the way they did (even if they wished for a different result), the storyteller has done their job of building up to a positive outcome.

Brainstorming Outcome Possibilities

One tip to try out in developing your positive outcome is brainstorming all of the outcome possibilities. Think of various emotions: happy, sad, angry, fearful, hopeful, surprised, confused, etc. Then, assign different endings to the story based upon each emotion. Consider everything that leads up to the outcome, and ask yourself which end has the most significant emotional impact on you. If you can't decide, consider presenting your ideas to a trusted individual who can tell you which end has the largest emotional impact on them. To try this out, let's reconsider the story of the couple who met on the bus, assigning different endings based upon each emotion we encounter.

Happy Ending

The man reads the love poems he wrote about the woman every day as she recovers in the hospital, and she listens and learns from him about how social anxiety has impacted his life. The two begin to brainstorm ways to shed light on individuals fighting physical and mental battles that are not evident from the outside. Soon after the woman is released from the hospital, they move in together, get married, and start a project called "Letters from the Invisible." In this project, they have people all over the world write letters about why they feel invisible, specifically concerning disabilities. They respond and help develop policies that are more inclusive and aware of the struggles people face.

Sad Ending

The woman reveals her condition to the man before she has her medical episode, and she breaks up with him. He does not yet reveal to her how much he loves her, or how hard it was for him to approach her, nor does he tell her about the letters he wrote. He begs her to stay, but she doesn't, convincing him it is for his good. When she has her medical emergency, her sister calls him, and he rushes to the hospital to be by her side. When she wakes up, she can't speak, but he tells her everything that he had been too afraid to share. He reads the letters to her every day and does not leave her side. On the day he tells her he loves her; she squeezes his hand three times in response. A few hours later, she dies. Although this ending is heartbreaking, there is still a sense of positive outcome because there is nothing left unexpressed, and the depth of true love rings true.

Angry Ending

The woman finally finds the courage to reveal to the man what she has been going through on her medical journey. As much as he tries to be there for her, he can't find it within himself to be able to support her, primarily because of everything he is dealing with on a psychological level. He ends up ending the relationship, at which point the audience will be angry with him and very concerned about her well-being. At this point, out of defiance, she discovers the importance of self-love and begins writing poetry about what it is like to live with an invisible illness and overcome the daily obstacles, especially as it pertains to love. She establishes a future for herself and becomes successful. The anger of him ending the relationship leads to clarity on her end, and she discovers something crucial about herself and her journey. Although the reader may feel angry at the situation, there is still a positive outcome in the message of self-love, independence, and overcoming obstacles.

Fearful Ending

After the woman's medical emergency, she and the man grow together, tell each other their stories, move in together, get married, and take all the other steps of the happy ending. However, in the fearful ending, perhaps the man's psychological health continues to worsen as the couple grows older, until he reaches a point where it is too difficult for him to talk, function, or live out his dreams with his wife.

Additionally, he may be unable to support her, and the task of defending him falls on her shoulders, even though she is still chronically ill, and they have grown older. Perhaps he eventually has to go into a care facility and loses recollection of who she is altogether. She has to move back in with her sister, and when she comes to visit him, he doesn't recognize her but achieves peace when she reads him the old letters he wrote her about "The Woman on the Bus." This ending may inflict fear in the audience because it shows how even when things seem happy at first, life is impermanent and there is always the risk of bad things happening and not going as planned. However, it also provides a solemn dose of reality, leading them to be more attentive and grateful in daily life.

Hopeful Ending

After the hopeful ending, the doctors tell the woman that they do not know how to figure out what is going on with her. She stops doing frequent doctor's visits and chooses simply to live in the moment with her love, making a difference in the world, and not being held back by her illness. Although it is unclear how long she will live, the audience can be filled with hope as she chases her dreams and pursues the fullest life possible despite the circumstances. This ending is more ambiguous and provides the reader with a sense of hope that the woman will survive, the couple will grow, and the world will continue to be changed by their legacy.

Surprising Ending

The woman wakes up after her medical emergency and has a realization about what she truly wants. She begins to understand that the thing she is truly looking for in life is the love she can provide to herself and how she can use her story to inspire other people. Although the man professes his love to her, she denies him, wishing him the best and telling him that they both should spend their time focusing on how to make others feel seen and recognize that the greatest kind of love is self-love.

They maintain a friendly relationship, but both pursue individual paths which are not focused on romance, but instead on self-healing and healing the world. This ending may also inflict feelings of anger in the reader, but ultimately, it is still a positive outcome that holds a more profound message and ties all previous events together.

Confusing Ending

An example of a well-done confusing ending would be one in which, after the woman's medical emergency, the couple takes the risk to move in together. They have no idea what they will do next or if either of them will live beyond the next day, but they choose to surrender to that and focus on being together. This ending may leave the reader feeling confused, wondering if either of them ever receives a diagnosis, if they die, or if they continue to struggle in society. It is important to address confusing endings with caution. Having a confusing end, and leaving the audience feeling lost as a result of an incohesive series of events, are two very different things.

Confusing endings are built up to by a sequence of logical events that lead to an open-ended outcome. This type of outcome is positive because it allows the audience to take the events of the story and what they know of the characters and draw their conclusions about what may have happened. This is a profoundly intellectual experience that requires an understanding of the story's primary message(s) and is sure to leave a long-term impact on the reader as they consider all the possibilities of what may have happened to the characters.

Chapter 7: Step 7 - Developing a Shining Moment

To share a great story is to give your audience a gift that can last them a lifetime. In many ways, storytelling is the gift that keeps on giving because it can be passed from person to person, continuing to form generations of people long after it is first told. Since the beginning of humankind, stories have been shaping reality as we know it and drastically changing the world's course and the ways we understand each other. As a storyteller, you have a major role to play in this process of bestowing gifts on humanity. Throughout this guide, we have explored many of the methods of developing top tier storytelling skills. In this final chapter, we will discuss one final element that is crucial to the storytelling process—developing a shining moment.

Central Character Dilemmas

No matter what your story's content is, or what main message you choose to express, your characters will be faced with conflict as the story unfolds. There will be times when your characters will be faced with difficult decisions, and sometimes, they may make the wrong decision. This not only creates a moral complication within the story and deepens the emotional experience, but it also creates a sense of integrity and sets expectations for the characters to live up to. Oftentimes, when a central character is faced with a difficult decision, they may choose the "wrong" option and be de-railed as they have to come to terms with their mistake and fix it.

Creating a Growth Experience

Your storytelling process should be like a rollercoaster ride in which your readers are emotionally invested and hanging on tight for what comes next. It is your job as the storyteller to take them on the journey with the characters. As your characters continue to grow and learn the lessons which are central to the theme of the story, your audience will learn and grow as well. Give them moments to root for the character, to hurt for them, and perhaps to feel angry or annoyed at them for making the "wrong" decisions. From here, you can build up to the "make it or break it" element of your story—the shining moment.

Creating Shining Moments that Stick

The shining moments are the things that tend to stick with us most about the stories we hear. Does your central character lead an army to victory after a vicious war? Do they learn the art of self-love after years of searching for romance? Do they die for a worthy cause? Do they recover from a history of addiction and pursue work in the field of providing help to other addicts? No matter what the shining moment is, it must be in direct alignment with the story's theme. The shining moment you determine for your character may vary depending on what you hope the audience will take away. For this reason, it is a good idea to play with ideas for shining moments in the same way you play with positive outcomes/endings. The decisions you make on these areas will shape the track of your entire story, and therefore, should be roughly developed before you get too far into the writing process itself.

Combining Shining Moment with Positive Outcome

The decisions you make about your shining moment go hand-in-hand with the idea of a positive outcome, as described in Chapter 6. Once you have determined the general emotional experience to take with your positive outcome, you can identify your shining moment within it. Let's take a look at the examples of each kind of outcome discussed in Chapter 6 for the story of the couple who met on the bus, and consider how the shining moments could vary for each one.

Happy Ending Shining Moment

In this example of a positive outcome, the shining moment is focused on both central characters. First of all, the man experiences a shining moment by overcoming his anxiety enough to tell the woman how he feels, sharing his deepest vulnerabilities with her through reading the letters. The two then experience a shining moment as a couple as they take everything that has happened to them and begin to develop a plan to help other people who have felt beaten down or unseen by society.

As they build a life together and create the legendary project "Letters from the Invisible," everything comes full circle. It leaves the audience feeling proud and inspired by the theme of the story and the way the characters have reacted in response to the difficulties they have faced.

Sad Ending Shining Moment

In this ending, the man still has a shining moment when he rushes to the hospital to be there for the woman even after she has broken up with him. He sets himself and his fears aside and does not leave her side, while also opening himself up to be vulnerable with her and share his heart through the reading of the letters. He demonstrates his shining moment by the acts of love shown while she is in the hospital and by eventually swallowing his fear to a point where he can finally tell her the truth—that he loves her. She joins in the shining moment at this point when she squeezes his hand three times to signify her love so that even once she has died the audience can walk away knowing that nothing was left unsaid.

Angry Ending Shining Moment

In this ending, the woman is the one with the most prominent shining moment, as she overcomes the challenge of being left after revealing the truth to the man about her medical journey. Although she is in pain, she makes the most of it, pursuing her dreams with all she has and making a change in the world on her own. She discovers self-love and begins to express herself creatively in a way that has incredible success. She speaks her truth about living with an invisible illness and how she overcame the obstacles she faced and learned how to adore herself and pave the way to her future. In this example, her clarity and self-discovery are the shining moments of the story.

Fearful Ending Shining Moment

In this ending, the man's shining moment of caring for and expressing his vulnerabilities to his wife while she was sick transitions into the woman's shining moment, of doing the same for him after he has begun to go downhill psychologically. Even though he can no longer support her in the way he once did, and she has to face the challenges of having him forget who she is and moving back in with her sister, she exhibits extreme dedication, support, and unconditional love on her visits when she reads him the letters from the past. Despite the incredibly difficult and scary circumstances, her strength prevails, and she manages to find gratitude and bring peace to her love every single day. This gives us a shining moment in which, even amid trial, heartbreak, and the fear of life's impermanence, love trumps all.

Hopeful Ending Shining Moment

With this ending, the shining moment is the woman choosing to live in defiance of her circumstances, choosing joy, gratitude, and the fullest life possible despite her mystery medical journey. She decides to place more of her energy in day-to-day life and how she can make the world a better place, as opposed to allowing uncertainty about her health and the future to hold her back. Her shining moment is, despite her life circumstances, living life to the fullest and understanding what the meaning of life is truly all about

Surprising Ending Shining Moment

In this ending, the woman once again is the character who experiences the larger shining moment. After her last medical emergency, she makes a powerful realization about what she is truly searching for in life, and that is the love that only she can provide for herself, and the legacy she can create by sharing her story in the world. She makes the bold decision to tell the man they should go their separate ways and pour their energy into building individual legacies, and that is precisely what happens. At this point, the shining moment ends with both of them on a journey of self-healing and changing the world.

Confusing Ending Shining Moment

The shining moment in this ending happens as the couple decides to take the leap and move in together. They surrender to their life exactly as it is and choose to make the best of it for as much time as they have left. During this time, the couple continues to grow in love with one another and realizes that daily life is a gift, and our presence in each moment is crucial.

Leaving Space for Evolution

What if you think you know what your shining moment will be, but as you develop the story, you find it takes on a mind of its own? If this happens, don't be alarmed. Although it is important to have a vague idea of what the shining moment will be to keep yourself on task and prevent audience boredom or confusion, it is certainly okay to adhere to the way the story changes after you have started writing. Give yourself the freedom to make adaptations as you go—just remember to keep revising to make sure you're still on track.

Conclusion

When you started this guide, you knew that storytelling was a universal talent—one which you desired to grow your skills in. Throughout the guide, you were provided with the ins and outs of storytelling, things to avoid, and tips to apply to keep yourself on track, keep your audience engaged, and arrive at a legendary shining moment. As you learned these methods, you also discovered the fact that storytelling is one of the greatest gifts you can give. Once you have gifted your audience with a good story, they may take it forward. Now that you understand the power held by storytellers, and how to exhibit that power, you have everything you need to be on your way.

You began this journey by uncovering the purpose of the story being told and how to organize and structure it. You discovered the importance of the 2 C's, character development, clarifying primary goals, and tying everything together throughout the story. Next, you learned methods of engaging your audience and keeping their attention throughout. You discovered the importance of storytelling as an emotional experience and how you can use personal narrative to achieve this and make your readers feel it. The guide went on to implement strategies for maintaining an element of surprise. You learned the importance of bringing things full circle with a positive outcome and creating a shining moment for the audience to take with them and continue to share — keeping your story alive for years to come.

Book 2: How to Write Fiction

---

7 Easy Steps to Master Fiction Writing, Novel Writing, Writing a Book & Short Story Writing

Jaiden Pemton

Introduction

There is a magic in storytelling that has been present and passed down from generation to generation. When it comes to writing fiction, you have the entire world at your fingertips, and you can create anything you desire. Fiction allows us to take elements of our knowledge, experience, and passions, and mold a reality for our own. As fascinating as this is, the task itself can be incredibly daunting. If you find your characters falling flat, your setting getting lost in the background, your point of view changes throughout the story, or your theme becoming lost in the chaos, you are not alone. When it comes to writing fiction, there are a lot of things to keep in mind in order to keep the reader engaged and be sure the story is being told in a way that is memorable, meaningful, and easy to follow.

While it can be difficult to discern the best way to channel story ideas into a cohesive fiction piece, the process of fiction writing doesn't have to be as overwhelming and chaotic as it may seem at first glance. All it takes is a deeper understanding of each of the elements of fiction writing. Also, the details that influence how each of those elements unfolds. This guide breaks down the details within each step of fiction writing, opens your mind to new possibilities, and helps you to come in touch with your goals for fiction writing.

The chapters of this guide will take you through each step of fiction-writing in a way that will help you check all the boxes and avoid common mistakes. Each detail is designed to keep you on track and answer any and all questions you may have about fiction writing. These sections contain all the information you need to develop well-rounded characters, a logical plot, an in-depth and meaningful setting, a suitable point of view, and a relevant and influential theme for each fiction story you write. Throughout the journey, you will find yourself discovering your own writing voice, and experimenting with

various styles of fiction writing until you find the one that is the best fit for you.

Each chapter is organized in an easy-to-follow, subtitled format with comprehensive examples of every tip, trick, and technique. This all-inclusive guide to fiction writing also contains a number of special fiction-writing secrets embedded throughout the text, which can help to develop your skills as a writer further. Whether you are aiming to write fiction stories based upon experiences in this world or another, this guide has all the tools you need and is sure to serve as the perfect guide to revolutionize your fiction writing experience.

Happy writing!

Chapter 1: Step 1 - Building Characters

Before you can begin to tell a story, you must determine who the people are that are enduring the story. It is the characters who make the story move—who draw the reader into a new world and make them feel a part of it. The most important part of character development is to make your characters feel entirely real. If the character seems flat, aloof, or unrelatable, your reader will not be able to create a connection with them, and they will entirely lose interest in the rest of the story. Therefore, developing real, raw, and complex characters should be in the forefront of your character developing process. Think back to when you were a child. If you ever walked away from a movie or finished a book and found yourself imagining what your life would be like as the characters, that means the characters were well-developed. Something about the way those characters were represented, even if they lived in a society, era, or lifestyle that was entirely different than your own, made you feel like you could put yourself in their shoes.

Additionally, real and raw characters are more likely to portray the deeper messages of the book because the reader will develop a sense of trust and compatibility with them.

Character Introduction

It is vital to introduce your character to the reader at the beginning of the story so they may begin to develop a strong initial connection. Certain hard and fast details like age, cultural background, nationality, voice, occupation, and markable physical qualities like tattoos, style of dress, beauty marks, or imperfections are important to establish an initial image in the reader's mind. Another way to set characters apart and create individual images for each of them is to give them a tag. Tags are notable qualities such as an accent, a particular piece of jewelry, a unique gesture or mannerism, or a passion unique to that character. If, for example, your protagonist is in love with a girl down the street who has black and white tattoos all the way up her arms, this is not only an initial point of interest but also a distinguishing element of that character to make them stick in the reader's mind and bring back throughout the story. Additionally, the significance of the girl's tattoos can lead to opportunities for dialogue between characters and a deeper representation of the girl's personality and life.

From the beginning, your reader should have enough details to have a distinguished image and voice in their head whenever a particular character enters the scene. Once you have introduced your characters, it is important to establish trust with your reader, giving them credit to use their own imaginations and develop a unique understanding of each character as they read the story. One of the most important elements of fiction writing is "show, don't tell." You should not have to provide a lengthy narrative summary to develop your reader's understanding of the characters. Rather, the character's background story, daily choices, internal dialogue, and the way they orient themselves in the world should speak for themselves.

Establishing Character Depth

After the initial introduction, your characters will continue to unfold into three-dimensional figures. Remember that character development involves creating an entire human being with a past, a present, and a future—you must be thorough. Although you may not reveal every single element of your character's past in the story itself, you must personally be aware of every single detail that composes that character and their experience. Basic descriptions of physical qualities and personality traits are not enough to establish depth. Take a piece of paper, and write out the elements of your character's life from their birth until the present moment. Where were they born? Who are their parents? What did their family unit (or lack thereof) look like? What sort of impact has this had on their development? What is the relationship status of this character? Do they work or attend school? Do they have any children? Who are the people in this character's circle; do they have a best friend? What are this character's hopes, dreams, skills, and talents? What most commonly produces an issue in their everyday life or stands in their way?

You should establish a personal awareness of what triggers anger, fear, grief, or trauma in this character, and why that is so. It is also important to assign a personality type to your character. Is this character a peacemaker who sometimes struggles to put their own needs first, or are they constantly ready to speak up, challenge authority, and fight until they are heard? Perhaps this character is a deep creative who feels largely misunderstood by the world, or a timid, rule-abiding personality trying desperately to find their own voice.

Making Characters Relatable

It is impossible to identify or empathize with any character who does not possess human qualities. This means you must have a basic understanding of human psychology, how people's brains work, and what causes people to react to things the way they do. If, for example, your character possesses superhuman strength, is kind at all times and never runs out of patience or energy, has no physical flaws, or never experiences emotional conflicts, your reader will not feel that they can relate. Humans are imperfect and flawed, and conflict is a regular aspect of our lives. It is important to keep this fact in mind when you approach fiction writing.

Your character should have flaws, just as every human being does. However, because your main character must possess some heroic qualities, you must ensure that these flaws are forgivable, identifiable, and easy to empathize with. It is important to dedicate plenty of time to define your character's flaws, how these flaws impact their lives, and how they move beyond (and in spite of) them. Your character will struggle, but they should never be portrayed as weak or cowardly. Although they have flaws, there should always be heroic qualities present that keep your reader engaged and rooting for character growth and success.

Growth as Expressed by the Character Arc

In terms of growth, it is vital to understand the "character arc". The character arc represents the path on which a character grows and changes throughout the story. Just as human beings are constantly changing as a result of what we learn and experience, so it should be for fictional characters. Throughout the story, great attention should be given to the character's inner dialogue. What keeps your character awake at night? Do they have any secrets? What is their largest fear, shame, and driving force? At the end of the story, what does your character know about themselves or the world that they did not know before? How has their life changed as a result of what has happened to them? How have they grown as a person? How do they approach the future?

In the book *The Alchemist,* for example, the young shepherd boy begins the book striving for something greater but feeling unsure of how to get there. Throughout the course of his journey to find the treasure, he is met with insights on his interactions with other people, the fire at the heart of every human being that can act as a guiding force, and the presence of omens to guide people towards that life purpose. His character develops until he has made the pinnacle observation of where to find the truths of life and oneself.

Making it Personal

When it comes to fictional character development, it can be helpful to take personal inspiration. Consider the complexities of your own life, personality, and those of the people you know. You can take the approach of changing several details of a personal experience to create a new circumstance. What are some ways that particular circumstance could have turned out? How do you wish it went? Could it have gone worse? In fiction, you have the freedom to base your characters off of real people in real experiences, while changing as many details as necessary to create your own story. We will take more about personification in later chapters.

Writing Exercise: Putting Yourself in Their Shoes

One of the greatest joys of writing fiction is the freedom to embody the characters you create. Whatever you dream of being—the villain, the heroine, someone of a different personal or cultural background, a mystical creature, a young child, a single mother, a soldier—fiction gives you the space to be that person. Every time you sit down to write on a certain character, take a few moments to close your eyes, breathe deeply, and truly become that character. At every twist and turn of the story, ask yourself, "what would I do if I were in this character's shoes right now?"

As you develop your characters, ask yourself which words you can use to summarize that character's personality most accurately. Are they bold and confrontational or shy and reserved? If the character is bold and aggressive, you may write about circumstances in which they stand up for the ones they love and fight for the underdog when no one else will. However, their confrontational nature may also get them into trouble when they grow passionate and have trouble controlling their abrupt reactions. Putting yourself in your character's shoes can guide the events of the story, as well as the character's growth. In the case of the bold and confrontational character, perhaps they feel that in order to be strong, they must not be soft in any way. Over the course of the story, their character arc may involve learning about the strength that lies in being soft and allowing their guard to come down sometimes. In the case of the shy and reserved character, their journey may involve learning the strength in their own voice and how to use it to influence change.

Establishing Character Credibility

A final important detail of character development is establishing credibility. Although fiction writing gives you the freedom to make your characters whoever you want them to be, you will not be able to develop them without some research fully. If you are writing a character who comes from a different personal or cultural background than your own, has a different passion or occupation than your own, or has experienced a tragedy that you have not. It is not enough to base their story off of simply what you imagine it might be like. To create a well-rounded character for your readers to fully understand and empathize with, you must literally put yourself in that character's shoes. One way to do this is by finding interviewees who have had similar experiences to your character and can answer questions to generate a deeper understanding. If you are writing on an ER nurse, for example, you could try calling into a local hospital and asking for an ER nurse who would be willing to book an interview about a day in their life. Begin by asking the interviewee to describe a typical day in their life, doing the things the character in your book will be doing. Develop several questions to serve as a guide, then follow up with further questions as the interview goes. Be prepared to be surprised and confront ideas you were not prepared for. All of those details are important to include in order to establish true character credibility.

Another great option is to go into an environment like that of which your character lives or works in. In the case of the ER nurse, you may want to try to schedule a day to go into that environment and shadow an ER nurse on their day at work. Take field notes of everything you observe. You may even find that you can draw further inspiration from the specific details of that setting and the people you see there. You can go into any neighborhood, classroom, landscape, or other environments with a journal and allow it to move you freely. Write down your observations and any feelings you experience in that setting, and channel them into the description of your characters and their lives.

Chapter 2: Step 2 - Shaping the Story Through Plot Development

As you take on the beginning steps of fiction writing, you will often find that plot development and character development happen subsequently at times. The plot feeds heavily off of the characters navigating through it. And how they develop from the start of the story to the end. When planning out the specifics of what happens in your story, there are several key questions to ask yourself. First of all, you should identify a primary sequence of events and how your characters change over time as a result of those events. What locations does each of these events happen in? How does each of these events contribute to the larger structure of the story? How does it do with the development of its characters?

The Importance of the 5 W's (Who, What, When, Where, Why)

The 5 W's are one of the most important clarifying factors of any story. You should establish straight away who the important characters are, where the story is unfolding when the story is unfolding, what situation the characters are in, and why they ended up there. The best stories are not only clear about each of these 5 W's; they also provide room for circumstances to change. You can further engage your reader by demonstrating changes in the who as your protagonist finds a new part of themselves and unlocks new strength. Another example of engaging your reader in the who of your plot is if one of the characters turns out to have an identity. They have been hiding that is revealed later on in the story. This may bring an element of surprise to the reader and cause them to shift their perspective. Perhaps the where may change as the protagonist gets a new job or moves to a new city. You can also change the what by detailing revelations your character has about what their true goal in life is. Take as much time as you need to generate thorough answers to these questions.

Plot Development Toolbox: Outlines, Timelines, and Storyboards

In the beginning stages, you may find it helpful to create an outline that provides a detailed summary of how the book flows and how each event is connected. It can also be helpful to create a comprehensive timeline of events in the novel, which can later branch off into separate chapters. Storyboards are an excellent tool to keep you on track as you move through each of the story's scenes. On note cards, post-it notes, or something similar, you can detail which of your characters will be involved in each scene, and what the main point of that particular scene is. You will then have the opportunity to reorder the scenes as the story develops until you end up with the most logical sequence. As you transition from the planning process to the actual writing, you should be able to describe what the story is about using only two sentences. Once you can do this, you know that your ideas are fully developed, and the story has a strong foundation on which to be built.

Plot Introduction (What's the Main Goal?)

As you begin to introduce your characters at the beginning of the story, you must also introduce the plot by making the reader aware of each character's main goals. Be specific in describing these goals. For example, it is not sufficient to say that your protagonist wants to be a writer in the future. What kind of writing does she want to do? Does she hope to live in a certain area? How do her dreams impact the way she envisions herself in the future? It is far better to say that she wants to be a famous poet, living alone in a mountain cottage, and traveling the world, than simply that she wants to be a writer. The main goal should be established as a driving force to the character's life—it is the most important thing to them. This goal will shape why the character chooses to act the way they do. What decisions do they make? How does their goal motivate them and define their daily life?

Be sure that any main goals you present are realistic and attainable. Remember, you want your characters to be established as human beings first and foremost so that the reader can relate to them and empathize with them. Leave room for the story to continue developing and for the main goal to expand and change after the protagonist is faced with conflict. Large-scale plot development should be fueled by the basic, everyday moments the characters experience. You can reveal a lot about the underlying themes of the story by giving small details such as how a character engages in dialogue or what sorts of simple actions they take (such as how they make their commute in the mornings or how they decorate their desk).

Exposition

This crucial introduction to the characters and their motivations occurs in the exposition. The exposition is the first part of plot development, in which characters are introduced within an established setting. There should be some explanation of the primary themes and main events of the story. The central conflict should be evident from the beginning, and it should draw the reader in and make them want to know what happens next. The exposition will introduce whether the structure of the story is linear or non-linear. Linear structure is chronological—it starts at the beginning and builds from there. Non-linear structure, however, drops a reader into a moment right in the middle of things. This gives the reader a chance to understand the central conflict in terms of what is going on. But not why it is happening. If the story opens with a woman next to her unconscious boyfriend at a hospital, the reader comes to know both characters and that they are in the hospital. But the readers do not understand how they got there. Non-linear structures can create added tension by introducing effects before causes, and this approach can be very engaging for readers, making them hungry for answers.

For the purpose of exploring these elements of plot, let's consider the classic story *The Three Little Pigs.* In this story, the exposition of the plot is when all three pigs are introduced in the setting of the countryside. It is clear in the beginning that each pig has one goal in mind: to build their own house. From the beginning, we know that one pig is building their house of straw, one is using sticks, and the third is taking their time to build a sturdy house of bricks. We are introduced to the main goals and potential themes from the very beginning when we see how the pigs who use straw and sticks are in a hurry to finish building so they can just have fun. The pig who uses bricks, however, is patient and takes the necessary time to develop a sturdy house that can endure much more. Due to its rudimentary nature as a children's story, this story follows the linear structure.

Rising Action

The rising action is the place where everything begins building up to the turn of events. This is where the reader will understand the why and the what that was introduced in the exposition. The protagonist will be faced with conflict, which will lead them to the realization that their immediate goal will not be as simple to obtain as they originally thought; then, the character must begin to establish a New Goal. The rising action portion of the book should be tense and engaging, and the reader should begin to understand everything that is at stake for the protagonist. Character-driven scenes can be used to demonstrate what is at stake. An example of this would be a mother who is trying to shield her daughter from finding out she has magical powers in order to protect her from being discovered by forces of evil who will use her powers for themselves. Character-driven scenes lead to intense action scenes that keep the reader on the edge of their seat, rooting for the main character's success.

In the example of *The Three Little Pigs,* the Big Bad Wolf is introduced as a dangerous character who wants to eat the pigs. He watches them build from afar, plotting when he will attack. It is at this point in the story that the reader understands the why behind the pig. The pig who chose to take the time to construct a sturdy house of bricks. When the big bad wolf arrives, the pigs who built their houses of straw and sticks are faced with conflict (the Big Bad Wolf trying to break in and eat them, then blowing their houses down). This leads them to understand that their immediate goal, to build their houses quickly and return to business as usual, is not as practical as they thought. This part of the story contains the intensity necessary in the rising action part of the plot as the story approaches the climax.

Climax

The climax, or turning point, is the point in the story where the protagonist realizes what they must do in order to resolve the conflict. This is the part where the main questions the reader has developed throughout the course of the story are answered. At this point, all of the tension and emotion that has accumulated throughout the first part of the story will be released. This is when the story switches from building conflict to conflict resolution, and it is often the most engaging part of the story. It is important to keep readers on the edge of their seats by making them question whether or not the protagonist will come out on top and experience a happy ending. There should be some element of doubt present—a moment where all seems lost before the protagonist rises above the challenge and ends up on top. The climax is the point where the reader develops an even deeper admiration for the main characters as they observe the characters making brave decisions, learning an important lesson, persisting through challenge, and rising above.

Using our *Three Little Pigs* example, we see the emphasis switch from the main goals of the straw and stick pigs to the main goal of the brick pig. This is the part of the story where the brick pig becomes the hero by allowing the other two pigs into the sturdy brick house. Tension continues to mount as the wolf tries to blow the brick house down and fails, then begins plotting another way in. At this point, the brick pig exhibits vigilance and quick-wittedness while preparing for the Big Bad Wolf's next move. When the Big Bad Wolf attempts to come down the chimney of the brick house, readers are left on the edge of their seats, wondering if he will get in and eat the pigs after all. However, in the end, the brick pig is too smart, and the Big Bad Wolf is encountered by a pot of boiling water in the fireplace. The Three Little Pigs are safe at last—a happy ending in which the characters learn an important lesson about being patient, thorough, and smart.

Falling Action

Everything that occurs after the climax is part of the falling action. The falling action should be in alignment with everything that has happened, leading up to that point, and it should feel inevitable. It must be directly tied to decisions and actions made previously, and the outcome should seem logical. This is the point where all the primary questions have been answered, and all conflicts have been resolved.

There are several versions of *The Three Little Pigs,* but one example of a falling action that can be seen in some of them is when the pigs engage in singing and dancing after the Big Bad Wolf has been defeated for good. As they dance around, carefree and enjoying themselves, the reader can see how the pig who made a house of bricks was right — patience is key. At this point in the story, all of the pigs are happy, safe, and unified together, and they are all benefiting as a result of the third pig's decision to build a sturdy house of bricks for protection, then place water on the fireplace to outsmart the Big Bad Wolf.

Resolution/Denouement

The final aspect of plot development is resolution or denouement. This draws all events, conflicts, and questions to a conclusion. This is the place where all of the loose ends are tied up by the lovers finally ending up together, the hero receiving recognition, or the adventurer returning home. This part of the book symbolizes a new, and generally improved, reality for all of the characters. At this point, the characters will have undergone great development as well and will have grown into wiser and improved versions of themselves who have successfully resolved the conflict they faced. This part of the story should be logical (do not introduce outlandish scenarios or new characters here) and leave the reader feeling satisfied.

The recognition the third pig receives in The Three Little pigs when the other two pigs express their gratitude for being protected and apologize for judging the third pig for working at a slower pace, is an example of resolution. At this part of the story, the reader can truly see how it all paid off and how the other two pigs have grown wiser and learned from their mistakes. Ultimately, the reader should arrive at this resolution feeling satisfied that all the pigs are safe, happy, and have learned a new life lesson.

The Use of Subplots

Although subplots are not the main idea of the story, developing subplots can be useful for supporting the main plot and highlighting the most crucial issues and themes at the heart of the story. An example of a subplot could be the protagonist's relationship with the shop owner down the street who always shows grace and kindness and holds space for people to share about their life issues. The development of this relationship over time could serve to drive in the story's key points about human relationships and a general understanding of the kinds of people the characters are.

Clarifying Questions: Did Your Plot do its Job?

As you approach the end of your story writing process, it is important to go back and ask yourself several important questions to ensure that you have stayed on track with what you wanted to express in the plot. Have the characters changed over the course of the story in the way you hoped they would? What were the key areas of growth or learning for the characters? What led them to change? Did they achieve their goals? Lastly, did you stick to the core themes of the story (for example, true love always prevails)?

Going back once more to *The Three Little Pigs* example, the goal of the story is that taking your time to think things through will benefit you later. We can see that this has been clearly demonstrated over the course of the story in the way the two pigs who did not take their time learning from the third pig, who did. This is an area of character growth and learning for the pigs. It is also an area of triumph for the pig who was not afraid to go against the grain. At the end of the day, the third pig's goal, to live in a house sturdy and safe from dangers like the Big Bad Wolf, has been achieved. The theme of the story has been achieved by demonstrating how patience and thinking things through led to a happy ending for the pigs.

Chapter 3: Step 3 - Defining the "Where" Through Setting

In order to draw your readers into the world you create in fiction; you must first have a profound understanding of what makes that world what it is. This is where developing a setting comes into place. When it comes to writing fiction, there is often much emphasis placed upon who the characters are, what they are doing, and what is happening to them and very little emphasis on the environment they are in. The setting is one of the most widely overlooked yet equally crucial components of fiction writing.

Basics of Setting: What to Do and What Not to do

Before setting out to develop your story setting, there are several things to keep in mind. First, when describing the setting, it is important to use all five senses. By describing exactly what the characters can see, hear, smell, taste, and feel, the reader will feel completely immersed in the story and where it goes next. The setting is not something that you can establish once and expect the reader to stay engaged throughout the rest of the book. It is important to spread setting descriptions out throughout the book in order to pull your reader into each moment truly. Whenever the plot is thickening or changing, and the character's actions need to be emphasized, that is a good time to provide new details of the setting.

While in-depth sensory descriptions of settings are crucial, there is a fine line between being thorough and over-describing. If you spend too long describing every tiny detail of the setting all at one time, your reader is sure to lose interest and become distracted. Not only this, but over-describing a setting may also stifle a reader's imagination, making it more difficult for them to envision the world in a way that is captivating to them.

Location, Context, Social Era, Lifestyle

Now that you are aware of how to approach the setting, let's talk about the details you'll need to provide in order to illustrate the bigger picture. First of all, you need to know the general location of your story. This involves the country, region, city/town, or planet (if your story takes place in another world). Once you have established a general location, you will break it down into smaller categories such as specific neighborhoods, households, or places of work or study. It is important to establish context around the social era the story is taking place in as well. If the story is happening during a post-war era, or in a city neighborhood that is being newly gentrified, those elements will greatly impact the journey. The journey of the characters and the unfolding of the plot. You must take into account any element of culture. What country, tribe, or community are your characters involved in? Do they have any special family traditions? What are the foods they eat? It is important to indicate the general social and political climates of the story, as well as how people interact with one another in different contexts.

Geography and Population

Geography is an element of setting that goes hand-in-hand with a location as it pertains to the natural environment. Does your story take place in a mountain village, off the coast of Mozambique, in a corner of East Harlem, or in a galaxy far beyond our own? You must make your reader aware of both natural geography (oceans, rivers, forests, mountains) and man-made geography (bridges, monuments, buildings, cemeteries). Also, to be taken into account with geography is the population of a given setting. The character's experiences are likely very dependent on how many people live in their area. The experience of a character living in a small town, versus a city with several million people, versus an isolated island, will all be vastly different.

Climate, Mood, Atmosphere

The climate of a setting goes along the same lines as its geography as well. It is important to establish the relationship between climate and people's moods and well-being. It is more common, for example, to see a relaxed and carefree lifestyle in a village community on the coast than in Seattle on the 200th cloudy day, or in the deep woods while a family struggles to survive during a harsh winter. The mood and atmosphere of a story are developed as the characters react to elements of their environment, including temperature, lighting, and other factors that can be detected by the five senses. Before each scene, be sure to take time to ask yourself what kind of mood you are striving to establish. What is the weather like? Is it sunny and serene, with puffy clouds in the sky? Or is it a gloomy day with whistling wind that makes the hairs on your arms stand up? If the story is occurring inside, what is the atmosphere of the room? Is it comfortable and cozy, or is there something unsettling about it?

Time of Year, Time of Day, Passage of Time

Time of year is another important element of setting, which includes seasons as well as important days. These days can be holidays, first days of work or school, or significant dates to the characters such as anniversaries, birthdays, dates of death, and dates of past historical events. Time of day is important for describing if events are happening at dawn, dusk, in the heat of the afternoon, or in the middle of the night. While it is not possible to take the reader on a moment-by-moment journey as it would be in real-time, it is absolutely crucial to account for elapsed time throughout the story. Flashbacks, foreshadowing, and in-between moments can all be used to allude to the passage of time and keep readers from becoming confused or feeling removed from the story.

Establishing Setting in Fictitious Worlds

In the cases of fantasy and fictitious worlds, you will have a bit more work to do in order to draw your reader in and make them feel connected with the setting (as it is a world they have never seen). Begin by creating the world your story is occurring on. Does it resemble earth in any way? What are the major differences? Establish the name of the world, as well as how its creatures live and function. What is the terrain like? One very helpful tip for establishing this fictitious world is to draw a map. After you have developed a map of this world, you can narrow things down and determine in which particular settings the plot will unfold.

Why is Setting Important?

One common misconception about the setting is that it is only the backdrop of the story. This is incredibly false. The setting is crucial to the development of a story because it includes everything that has to do with how the characters navigate through space, time, and social environments. Think about the places in your own life where you spend the most time, for example. If you spend most of your time on a college campus, it is likely that you have a favorite meal in the cafeteria, a favorite faculty or staff person who you look forward to talking to a favorite tree or bathroom stall, and a favorite place to study. It is also likely that there is a building or room that you rarely enter because it is rumored to be haunted, or because the meanest or creepiest staff or faculty person works there. This is just one example of how setting impacts the way we orient in the world and why it is so crucial to creating a good piece of fiction writing. Every component of the story setting is essential to building the mood and plot of the story. As well as how the characters grow and change within each context. Your setting should be clearly described using literary devices and descriptive language that can clearly draw a picture in your reader's mind to help them envision the environment.

When story setting is done right, it will help the plot to flow from one event to the next clearly and realistically. The story setting should align with the plot of the story. For example, if you are writing about a young musician who is struggling to get by and make it big in New York, you will want to describe the setting of his closet-sized apartment. Also, the streets where he feels unseen and the subways he falls asleep on every day as he travels home from the barista job that barely pays the bills. A rustic, mountain setting would not make sense for this plot.

Further Benefits of Setting

The setting also creates a sense of unity between the characters and the plot by describing why the characters do what they do and which elements of their environment lead them to be in certain situations. Additionally, setting draws the reader in to feel like they are truly in that place with the character, experiencing the same narrative and emotions.

The setting should be aligned with the main characters throughout the story. Going back to the example of the young musician. If his conflict is being withdrawn and not having the confidence to pursue his dream, it is likely he keeps his eyes down on the city streets and attempts to sit alone and mind his own business on the subway. However, if he is outgoing and willing to talk to anyone or do anything to fulfill his dream, even when that means failure, it is likely he is trying to talk to everyone and drop his name in any context he can. He may be trying to instigate conversations about his music with everyone he comes across and is likely to seize any opportunity to perform (at parks, in cafes, in bars, etc.). In this case, the character's conflict would not be a lack of confidence, but rather, lack of opportunity or being noticed.

Establishing Setting Credibility

Just as it is important to establish credibility with character development, it is important to develop that same credibility with the development of particular settings. If you are trying to describe a real place that you have never been, it is crucial to do research on that place to make sure what you are describing is geographically and culturally accurate. If it is a place you can visit in person, that is the best way to get a real-life understanding of the setting. However, this is not always logistically possible. In those cases, you can make use of media resources such as Google Earth, YouTube, newspaper clippings, images/photographs, and encyclopedias. You may also do the same thing you did in the stages of character development, where you visit particular settings and take field notes on what you observe.

Chapter 4: Step 4 - Selecting a Point of View

The point of view of fiction writing is the type of narration you choose to tell the story. When it comes to selecting a point of view for your fiction story, you have several options to choose from.

First-Person Point of View

The first-person point of view adopts the perception of a character, generally the main character, of a fiction story. This point of view records everything as it is witnessed and understood by the character, and uses pronouns such as I, me, and mine. This point of view is useful for giving the reader a closer look inside the mind of the character, letting the reader know exactly how they think and feel and allowing for a more personal connection between the reader and the character. This close connection is a major benefit to using the first-person point of view. One disadvantage is that you may not be giving your reader a well-rounded view of the setting and the other character's perceptions of things. This point of view is more personal but also more limited.

Second-Person Point of View

In the second-person point of view, the narrator speaks directly to the reader and adopts pronouns such as you, your, and yours to tell you your own story. In fiction writing, second-person is most commonly used to guide the reader through interactive books.

Third-Person Objective Point of View

Third-person objective point of view is when a character serves as the narrator of the story but without any insight into their personal thoughts, feelings, and perception of what is going on. This point of view aims for neutrality through the use of third-person pronouns, and it is designed to be unbiased and give the reader the freedom to interpret what they are reading freely without the emotional response of the narrator.

Third-Person Limited Point of View

Third-person limited point of view uses both third-person pronouns and insight into a particular character's emotions and perception of the world. In this point of view, all characters will be referred to in third-person, but only one (usually the main character) will be followed throughout the story from start to finish.

Third-Person Omniscient Point of View

Third-person omniscient point of view is focused on giving the reader a point of view similar to that of a godly figure, looking down on everyone else and seeing what is happening. This point of view provides deep insight into the personal lives of several characters throughout the book, not just one character. In order to write in this point of view, you must be prepared to provide details of the emotional states, inner dialogues, perceptions, and actions of multiple characters.

Dialogue vs. Narration

When thinking of how to write a point of view, you must understand how to use the tools. The tools of both dialogue and narration. Even if the narrative is being written in third-person, first-person pronouns are still used when dialogue is occurring between characters. This is why it is crucial to symbolize every phrase of dialogue with quotation marks to set it apart from the rest of the text.

Point of View Toolbox: Moods and Dimensions

There are several tools available to you when deciding which point of view to use in a piece of fiction writing. Begin by asking yourself what type of story you are writing, and which sort of mood you hope to create. If you are writing a story designed to be suspenseful, you will be better off writing from a first-person perspective, as it is more limited and will inevitably create more tension. However, if you are writing a fantastical story about another dimension, you may choose to write from several third-person perspectives in order to give the reader a better understanding of the world.

Using Your Own Voice

The point of view you choose is also largely dependent on the journey of finding your own distinct style and voice to use in your writing. In order to develop your own strong writing voice, be sure to pay close attention to the differences in voices and points of view in the fiction stories you read. Ask yourself how you perceive different points of view differently. Which one sticks with you the most as a reader? While it is helpful to use the voices of other writers as inspiration, it is important not to attempt to imitate any other author's voice or force yourself to use any particular point of view. Trust your instincts. You know your story better than anyone!

Clarifying Questions: Observation vs. Participation

Several important questions to ask yourself before beginning are as follows. First of all, do you want your narrator to be involved in the events they tell about? Perhaps they are simply an observer of those events or are serving to reconstruct distant events with their narration. Is the narrator far removed from the story, or is there a lot at stake for them personally in the way things unfold? Lastly, is the narrator credible in telling the story? Can your reader trust that they have enough information and experience to portray the story accurately?

Chapter 5: Step 5 - Defining the "Big Idea" Through Theme

When it comes to fiction writing, every story must have a deeper meaning. When the reader reaches the end of the story, what is the message or topical knowledge they will be taking away? If your story lacks a theme, it inevitably will be lacking the ability to establish meaningful connections between the characters and the plot, and the story itself will lack significance or memorability. The theme is a central element of fiction writing; it answers the question, "What is this story *really* about?". Before you proceed with a piece of fiction writing, you should be able to summarize the main purpose of your story in one sentence. One important distinguishing factor is that theme is not the same thing as the moral of the story. The moral of the story is a lesson the author wants the reader to take away, while the theme relates more heavily to the deeper significance of the story.

Major Themes in Fiction Writing

The most powerful themes are generally those which appeal to common interest or understanding. The theme "good trumps evil" is one of the most common themes in literature, which expresses that even when the battle is challenging, forces of good always come out on top at the end of the day. The theme of power struggles and dynamics are also popular, and such themes typically demonstrate that one must have secret powers or approaches in order to achieve dominance. A common theme is one that claims the freedom of humans and the challenges of living in a society that tries to limit that freedom. Contrarily, there is a common theme that expresses society as the saving grace. That protects humans from their natural, animalistic wickedness.

Determining Your Theme(s)

Choosing a theme depends heavily on the general audience you are writing to, as well as the genre you are writing in. For example, the writings of romantic novelists would revolve around themes of love. Begin by determining the broad themes you plan to discuss (love, loss, power, loneliness, family, coming-of-age, self-discovery, mystery, the pursuit of happiness, etc.). You may determine that you want to write a cross-over of several themes, for example, the relationship between the pursuit of happiness, loss, and self-discovery. One way to maintain relevance to the theme is to base it heavily on your characters, setting, or plot. For example, if your protagonist is a professional female swimmer training to qualify for the Olympic team, your themes could have to do with competition, drive, the sport of swimming as a whole, the challenges that face women in athletics, or any combination of those. Ultimately, the theme is a summary of all the primary ideas of a story. Many great stories explore a variety of topics and subtopics, but it is important not to go so broad that your reader gets lost. A good rule of thumb is to select anywhere between two and five primary themes that your story will focus on. This will help you avoid getting off track and will keep your reader engaged. Lastly, although themes will vary between genres and intended audiences, it is important to select themes that are relatively universal and can appeal to people of all races, genders, cultures, lifestyles, ages, etc.

Thematic Statements

Thematic statements based upon opinions or moral discoveries the characters express throughout a piece of fiction writing which communicate a deeper message to the reader. The thematic statement is what combines and summarizes the main topics of the book in a brief phrase. For example, if the themes of a book are love and equality, the thematic statement could be "love your neighbor as yourself." Thematic statements demonstrate how the theme plays out in the world. After you know what your thematic statements are, you can stay on track with the larger purpose of your story and eliminate the details which don't support that larger purpose. It is important to keep character arc in mind when developing thematic statements in order to draw the reader in with a sense of humanity. Thematic statements can be present in everything from the character's backgrounds to their current internal conflicts. When writing about your character's experiences, it is vital to ask yourself, "How is this experience going to impact the reader? What message is the reader going to take away from this?"

The Use of Motif

A motif is a symbol, structure, or literary device that is recurring throughout a piece of fiction writing. Geography is one primary example of a motif. The themes in a story about a girl living on a Polynesian island and a teenage boy growing up in Baltimore, for example, would be very different. The elements of geography can play strongly into the reiteration of the theme throughout a story. Another common motif is the weather, and how changing weather patterns can represent a change in mood and expression of the theme.

The Use of Symbol

A symbol is a particular object, image, figure, or character that represents a deeper meaning. An example of a symbol is the bow and arrow Katniss uses in *The Hunger Games*. While on the outside, this is an object used in battle, it is also a symbol that represents the depth of Katniss' stealth, skill, precision, and courage.

The Relationship Between Theme and Character Development

As previously mentioned, a large part of theme development is dependent upon the character arc. It is vital to consider how the character's experiences, opinions, and morals relate to the overarching theme of the story. When considering the timeline of scenes and character interactions, it is important to ask yourself how they all contribute to the overarching theme. If your theme is "the concept of marriage," for example, and is focused on a young woman learning the lessons about marriage that the other women in her family never learned. It makes a lot of sense to provide a scene exploring her relationship with a single mother character who left her husband after he was unfaithful.

Staying on Track

One of the biggest benefits of summarizing your primary themes from the beginning is that you can refer to it as a guide throughout the rest of the process (and subsequent development of motifs, symbols, and characterization). There is nothing worse than a piece of fiction writing that jumps from one scene to another in a chaotic manner that leaves the reader with questions and leaves them unable to identify the point of the story. Establishing your main themes ahead of time can help you avoid adding secondary characters, subplots, and random details that do not relate to what you are trying to convey. This skill, also called "cutting the fat," is necessary for keeping your reader from becoming lost, frustrated, or bored. Another useful tip for staying on track is to incorporate the primary theme(s) into your outline process, so you can have extra assuredness that each scene you write is relevant.

Because the theme is so dependent on other elements of fiction, such as the characters, plot, and setting, it is rare that writers are able to understand their theme from the beginning fully. Although you do want to establish primary themes to serve as a general guideline throughout the writing process, you may find that your theme will shift slightly as you go. If this happens, you must be prepared to re-evaluate and make adjustments accordingly to ensure that everything still flows.

Out of the Box Tip for Theme Writing

As previously mentioned, it's good to be able to summarize what your story is going to be about, and what some of the primary topics are, before you begin writing. That being said, many writers may find it inhibiting on their writing process to try to determine the theme before the story has even begun to take its course. In some instances, you may find it helpful to give yourself a brainstorming session in which you write down all of the possible topics and theme possibilities that lie within your story idea. You can loosely tie the primary topics into your planning process to keep you on track, but allow yourself some flexibility to let the main theme(s) of the story appear as you go. Although you will begin with some general ideas of what you want to express and what you want the reader to take away, it is a great idea to let the process guide you into creating a more concrete definition of your theme. Allow yourself to move with the flow of the story and watch how your theme(s) appear to you.

Chapter 6: Step 6 - Developing Style and Finding Your Voice

The writing world is brimming with possibilities for self-expression and stylistic variation. The voice and style you develop in your fiction writing allows you to create worlds all your own, which can serve as reflections of your inner world and personal aspirations. When it comes to developing your personal voice and style in fiction writing, there are several important things to consider. This chapter will explore the most crucial elements on the journey of finding your personal style and voice.

"Show, Don't Tell" with Style and Voice

As previously mentioned, it is important to leave room for the reader's imaginations by describing scenes with enough detail to both draw the reader in and inspire them to draw their own mental pictures. However, when it comes to developing style and voice, the way you choose to "show" is crucial. You should try to think outside the box when generating descriptions that stray from the typical perspectives. Ask yourself, "how can I apply my own personal twist to this perspective?" Another tip is to utilize expressive vocabulary. When using common adjectives, such as "beautiful" or "exciting," try searching for synonyms that can express the same thing in a more colorful way.

Determine What Makes You Unique

Every person sees the world in a different way. Perspectives are formed through life experiences, and because every person has a different story, every person has a unique perspective. No matter how insignificant you may feel your perspective is, it is guaranteed that there are elements of your perspective that can provide a new way of understanding the world to your readers. A good starting question when it comes to defining your personal voice and style is: "what makes me unique?" You may find it helpful to create a list of things that contribute to your perspective and who you truly are, from which to draw your personal style in writing. If you are a typically "romantic" person, allow that perspective to infiltrate your writing and create romantic storylines with your own unique twist. While your unique qualities may be as broad as a particular personality type or passion, they may also be narrow, such as your quirks, habits, guilty pleasures, strange fears, special objects, obsessions, or what brings you comfort. Allow the unique qualities you notice in yourself and other people to play a role in the way you detail the characters in your story. Perhaps you are writing about a character who wears glitter on their eyelids every day, has a nervous habit of shaking their pen when they or thinking, or who has a trademark way of greeting people. As mentioned in the Character chapter of this guide, such qualities are endearing and help the reader to build a personal connection with the characters in fiction writing.

Be Authentic

When you allow yourself to be completely authentic in your writing, you will quickly distinguish yourself as a writer. Some writers are known for writing with an element of suspense. At the same time, others write from a mystical perspective or explore the depths of the feminine. The sign of pure and engaging authenticity is to draw readers in so far that they forget what they are reading is fabricated. Over time, this engagement will lead to increased fiction writers developing their own unique presence in the writing world and becoming known for what they bring.

Be Original

Another crucial element to establishing your style and voice is to avoid clichés. If you are trying to imitate another storyline or style of writing, your writing will be dry and unoriginal, and it will ultimately lose the reader's interest. It is important to trust your own experiences and perspective enough to let it guide your writing process and avoid clichés. If you find yourself writing a phrase or following a storyline that seems like something you have heard before, it is a good idea to choose another direction to travel in.

Activating the Senses

One of the key elements of discovering your voice and personal style is to integrate sensory experiences into your writing. In order to draw your readers into the story, you must write in a way that illicit emotion and floods your reader with imagery to keep them engaged. To appeal to your reader's senses, you must write in a way that appeals to your own. When illustrating a scene, ask yourself what the character sees, what they hear, what they smell, and what they feel. As human beings, we are all attuned to different details of daily life. This personal attunement gives writers the ability to describe two very similar experiences in a completely different way, thus immersing the reader in a sensory experience unique to that author's perception of things. Allow your personal attunement to certain things to fuel your writing process and set you apart.

Spicing Things Up with Metaphor

A great way to unleash your creative side in fiction writing is to create metaphors out of everyday objects. This exercise can be applied to any object in your line of vision. Ask yourself about the backstory of that particular object, giving it a past, present, and future. Ask yourself, "What could this object stand for beyond its general purpose?" Consider, for example, a chipped coffee mug on the shelf of a thrift store. Day after day, people come in shopping for mugs, but every time they pick up this particular one, they end up putting it back because it's chipped. When someone eventually decides to purchase the mug in spite of the chip, this could serve as a representation of giving new chances and finding the value in brokenness.

The Importance of Intimacy

The more you invite the reader into a written experience, the more of an impact your writing will have on that reader. Your descriptions of setting and character should include minute details, which can help place the reader even deeper in the story and help them to feel like they are part of it. Seemingly insignificant details, such as the sound of the wind rustling and the branches of a tree brushing against the upstairs window, help the reader to put themselves in the character's shoes and experience the emotions the character experiences. Intimate details are another tool for distinguishing your writing style and truly bringing the reader into your world.

How Personal Experience Influences Voice

A common misconception among writers is that in order to generate fiction, you have to stay far away from any experiences that resemble your own. In reality, quite the contrary is true when it comes to fiction writing. Personal experience can serve as an excellent starting line for the journey of a fiction story. From here, you can draw inspiration from real people, emotions, life memories, and personal philosophies. Writing from this place creates space for empathy and authenticity in the story, which is sure to draw readers in and allow them to build an emotional connection with what they read.

Not only can you base some characters, elements of plot, setting, or theme, off of things you have experienced in your life, fiction also gives you the freedom to change details or elaborate in any way you choose! In fiction writing, you have the opportunity to use your personal life as a basic guideline, then let your imagination get to work in carrying the rest of the story. There is plenty of room for imagination and theoretical situations in relation to personal experiences, and the best fiction writers take advantage of this and allow it to influence their personal style and voice. Because every person's life is unique, so then can the way those experiences impact their writing.

Practice Writing Every Day

Coming to terms with personal experiences, memories, dreams, and philosophies is not a simple process. Humans beings are incredibly complex and constantly changing based upon what happens in their lives. One of the best ways to sift through experiences and find what you strive to express in your writing is by participating in writing every single day. When you sit down to write, try to do so without any expectations or plans in mind. Allow yourself to free-write without paying attention to any of the typical rules of writing. Allow your soul to pour out on the page, then allow yourself to be inspired by what comes from it. Over time, you will begin to notice recurring themes, philosophies, and passions, making an appearance in what you write about. Your free writings can serve as inspiration for the situations your fiction characters experience and the lessons they learn.

Chapter 7: Step 7 - Uncovering the Secrets of Good Fiction Writing

Now that you have covered each of the elements of fiction writing. You are almost ready to be on your way. However, any writer can follow the tips and information provided in definitions of each element of fiction. It is not by simply following the previous steps that you will become a strong and memorable fiction writer. In order to become truly distinguished, there are a few secret techniques to bear in mind.

1. Read, read, read. The more you indulge in personal reading endeavors, the more you will be able to identify the elements of fiction in practice. You will become familiar with the literary devices, style, and voice used by various authors. Pay attention to how certain stories make you feel and what you take away, and approach each of your own projects with the energy you hope to make your reader experience and what you want them to learn.

2. Dare to ask yourself, "What if?" and "What next?" Dare to dream about what you can create in your fictional world. If 'X' happens, what will happen to 'Y'? Give yourself space to think of all possible outcomes.

3. Take risks and immerse yourself in new environments. If you stay in the same place, doing the same thing, the writing you can base upon your personal experiences may begin to dwindle. Challenge yourself to try new things and visit new environments, and take notes each time you do. How might the observations of this new environment create a unique story idea?

4. Give yourself time to soak in the process. As writers, it is easy to feel a rush to get new stories generated as quickly as possible. This can be a critical mistake. In order to create a story that will stick with the reader, bring joy to your soul, and enrich your experience as a writer and a human being, you need to have the patience to let yourself ruminate in the writing process. This can come by way of sitting in quiet and pondering past memories and experiences of your life, which are fueling your stories, daydreaming about mystical worlds from which your story settings are drawn, or simply sitting at the moment and letting images and ideas flow freely onto the paper. Not only will giving yourself time and being present make your personal experience more enjoyable and lifechanging, but it will also refine your story and make it a true masterpiece.

5. Aim to write what has never been written before. Every writer has the capacity within themselves to create something

completely unique using their personal style and voice, but this takes courage. You must be vulnerable with the parts of yourself that long to come to the surface. Allow yourself to engage with them and let them flow forth in your works. Learn from your own process, be inspired by what comes. This is the only way to inspire others with your writing truly.

6. When you are describing scenes in fiction writing, pay attention not only to the descriptive words you use but how they flow together. Language has the ability to create rhythm with the way it flows together. Read your descriptive sentences aloud, changing words as needed until the rhythm and sounds reflect the mood.

7. Maintain an obligation to yourself. Although the goal of a writer is always to keep readers engaged, the primary goal at the end of the day should be to yourself. How can you write the stories that are on your soul? How can you say the things that you have been given the words, experience, and passion to say? At the end of the day, what your writing does for you personally is the most important thing.

8. Life is about choices, and life stories are no exception. Before setting out to write any story, consider the series of choices the characters will make. Why do the characters make certain

choices, and what impact do those choices have on how the story unfolds?

9. Determine particular "writing spaces" for yourself. Each time you set out to write, ask yourself where you need to be. You may take inspiration from writing in a garden, on a rooftop, in a junkyard, next to a country road, hunkered at a corner table of your favorite coffee shop, or settled at a writing desk you have created for yourself with things that inspire you. No matter where it is, make sure that you are in a space where your surroundings can inspire you and put your mind and spirit in the place they need to be.

10. Just get started. You may find yourself writing ten, fifty, or several hundred pages that don't end up going anywhere. That is part of the process. The hardest part of creating a fiction story is often simply choosing to get started. Decide to do that, and give yourself grace and patience as you observe where the process goes from there. Mistakes are a crucial part of the process, and you often have to sift through a lot of ideas and type many words before realizing where you are really trying to go.

Conclusion

Throughout this guide, you were provided with the ins and outs of fiction elements, including the basic elements, things to avoid, and tips to apply to your writing process. At this point, you not only have an interest in writing fiction that inspired you to start these 7 steps, but also the tools to embark on the journey that is fiction writing.

At the beginning of this guide, you learned how to develop characters with whom readers can relate and establish emotional connections. You learned how to add depths to characters and to make their personal growth journey engaging for the reader. Next, you learned about the elements of the plot, and how to prepare your story by establishing a character's main and new goals, conflict, and eventual resolution that leaves the reader feeling satisfied. You learned that setting is not just something that sits in the background of the story, but rather an incredibly dynamic force in the way the story plays out. You learned how to discern between the various points of view and how to select one based on your purposes. You then explored the possibilities of theme, and how to stay on track with what your story is truly about. After this, you examined how to cultivate your personal writing style and voice, largely depending on your past experiences and personal values. Lastly, you were provided with ten out-of-the-box secrets for improving your fiction writing.

This guide is not the endpoint of your journey to fiction writing— it is just the beginning. Now that you have familiarized yourself with the elements and secrets of fiction writing, you can continue to use this guide as a map; you refer back to throughout your process. Now is your time to change the world through the worlds you create in fiction writing.

Book 3: How to Write Content

7 Easy Steps to Master Content Writing, Article Writing, Web Content Marketing & Blog Writing

Jaiden Pemton

Introduction

When it comes to content writing, it is crucial to be aware of your audience, the needs they have, and how the content you are writing can satisfy their needs and positively impact their lives. This guide will show you how to develop engaging content which will leave your readers feeling satisfied and anxious to come back for more.

In an ever-changing world, there are millions of types of content. Because of this, it can be difficult to set your content apart and prove to readers why they should engage with it as opposed to the other competitors. Within each field of content writing, you can expect hundreds, if not thousands of different perspectives, calls to action and approaches. For this reason, it is crucial to have all the necessary information, know how to talk to your audience, and develop skills that set you apart and help you to achieve the necessary amount of engagement.

This guide will explore the importance of identifying your audience, defining your purpose, and writing content that will excite them and move readers to action. You must understand the logistical necessities of content writing, such as how to present the main ideas, write your conclusion, check your evidence, and edit yourself for technicality purposes. You will also understand how to use your own passion and voice as a way to develop a following surrounding your content, and give readers the feeling of importance within your niche.

This guide will provide you with mistakes to avoid, such as being too broad or narrow, boring your readers, or getting off-topic. You will learn how to avoid cliches and answer all of your reader's questions as they read. You will discern how to check every box in terms of audience questions, concerns, and desires, showing them what they need and how your content can help them get there.

This guide has everything you need to write effective content in a comprehensive step-by-step reference format. You will be exposed to every piece of in-depth knowledge necessary to appeal to your audience, provide the right information, and present a clear call to action. Additionally, you will understand how to distinguish the content you write from other content in your niche, and develop a feeling of reliability and engagement from your readers.

The chapters of this guide will take you through each step of the content writing process to help you avoid common mistakes and develop the process that works best for you and your content. Each chapter is designed with great detail to help you stay on track and address any questions or concerns you have along the way.

Chapters are easy-to-follow with examples of tips, tricks, techniques, and things to avoid. No matter what you are aiming to advertise through your content writing, or who your audience is, this guide has all the tools you need and is sure to serve as the perfect guide to revolutionize your content writing experience.

Happy writing!

Chapter 1: Step 1 - Writing for Your Audience

When it comes to writing content, you must be specific when choosing what information will make it to the page. This decision is heavily dependent on the audience, and the purpose your content aims to fill for a particular audience. Audience interest levels will determine the sorts of statistics, facts, personal narratives, observations, testimonies, and research you should present to your readers. The way you speak about an election process to a room of second graders, for example, is much different than how you would speak about it to a high school civics class or a room of Political Science majors. Understanding the audience is crucial to determining your tone, language, and the general complexity of a particular topic. The tone you select will shape your content and serve the purpose of keeping the audience engaged.

Knowing Your Audience

When it comes to delivering your content, you must have the correct information about your audience to ensure they will be interested and impacted by what you have to say. Consider the election example again. If you are presenting information to a classroom of second graders, you will need to use simple, image-based language and put things into terms that younger children will understand. If you're writing to a high school class, you should assume they have a bit more knowledge due to more experience, but you should not assume that they are experts on the topic.

Advanced figure charts, specified jargon, etc. may not be familiar to these students and may likely end up turning them off. If you're writing for an audience of Political Science majors, you can assume they have higher levels of expertise in the topic and will be in search of more in-depth statistics and terminology. By knowing the level of knowledge, interest, and life experience your audience has ahead of time, you will be able to create much more meaningful connections with them.

Visualizing Audience Reactions

The audience—individuals who will read your content—are one of the major determining factors in how you should develop it. You must have enough information about your audience to visualize their reactions, questions, and what they expect from you. You should have an acute awareness of your reader's interests, hopes, problems, goals, and general characteristics. This knowledge is also important when it comes to digital followers, including unintended readers who may stumble across your content. While invisible readers should not be the major determining factor in the content you write, you should keep some awareness that they may come across your content.

Obtaining Audience Demographics

When it comes to gathering information about your audience, there are several elements to consider. The first element to consider is demographics. Demographics are the data that revealed factors such as age, ethnicity, gender identity, sexual orientation, religious identity, socioeconomic status, and cultural beliefs. Most content writing assignments require an understanding of audience demographics in order to determine what needs to be said and how to say it.

Considering Level of Education

Another element of audience information to consider is the level of education. This applies in the earlier example of writing election content. When audience members have a higher level of education, they will be hungry to read a formal and elevated style with in-depth information and terminology. Conversely, if you are writing to a group of high school students, you will need to be more relaxed and avoid using terms that will cause readers to get lost.

Determining Prior Knowledge

Prior knowledge is also important when deciding how to write your content. You must be aware of what the audience already knows about the topic. Are there any terms or concepts you need to define to make sure your reader understands what's being discussed? How can you feed the knowledge they already have and teach them something new, without going too far over their heads? As a content writer, it's your job to make reasonable assumptions about what your readers already know in order to avoid boring or confusing them.

Defining Reader's Expectations

Lastly, you must be aware of your reader's expectations. What will your audience expect to get out of reading this piece of content? What can they expect to learn? They may approach your content with preconceived notions about the topic and the impact they hope it will have. Additionally, they may have expectations for technicalities like grammar, terminology, formatting, and font. Be mindful of how you title your content, as this will be one of the major determining factors to shape your audience's expectations.

Determining Content Purpose

Once you have determined your audience demographics, education, prior knowledge, and expectations, you can begin to make decisions about the purpose and tone of your content. The purpose of writing a piece of content serves to answer the question *"why?"* If you are writing a piece of content about an election, geared towards an audience of college students, perhaps your purpose is persuading college students to vote. Perhaps your purpose is to create a sense of customer satisfaction in terms of readers feeling pleased with the content they engage with. Or you may seek to fill the void readers feel when they believe businesses do not accurately understand their needs. You may also seek to ease the frustration readers feel by making them feel understood and like the content they are seeing is relevant to their needs. As you develop your purpose, make sure to familiarize yourself with marketing tactics, areas of customer satisfaction and dissatisfaction, and the importance of timing.

Attracting Audience Attention

After you have developed an understanding of who your audience is and the purpose your content will serve, it's time to attract the reader's attention and keep them interested. The world is overflowing with content, and it can be overwhelming to create quality content that stands out. That said, there are a number of tips that can make you a content writing expert in no time at all.

Asking Questions and Sharing Extra Information

Your audience will not be engaged with your content if they don't feel like it is speaking to them. One of the best ways to interact with your audience is by asking questions. Statistically, asking questions of your readers makes them feel important and connected to the content. Asking questions makes readers use their brains to decide whether or not they agree with you, and if they do, this is a good sign that they are being persuaded. It can also be useful to share information about topics related to your content, which will give readers further reasons to engage. Ask yourself how you can produce content that readers will find valuable and lead them towards further action. By sharing further related topics, you can create a sense of community surrounding your audience's values and interests.

Making Use of Written and Video Reviews

Reviews are another excellent way to keep audience members excited and engaged with your content. As a content writer, you should be aware of the best services and resources within your niche, and you can use this knowledge to your advantage. You can gain credibility as a content writer by writing reviews of products, apps, services, and other resources to share information with your audience.

In doing this you can create excitement over tips, advice, recommendation, benefits, and things to stay away from. By that same token, video interviews are another trend that can help you develop yourself as a content writer. You can support the content you write by conducting video interviews where people share their thoughts on the topic at hand. If you can't do interview videos, written interviews can work just as well, and readers will enjoy gaining new information and insights from other readers in the community.

Knowing Your Niche

If you are writing for a particular audience, such as within an academic field or business niche, you should seek to share insights with your readers. What knowledge do you hold about this niche that your readers don't? Take the opportunity to share your insight, along with comprehensive lists of tips and tricks your readers will be excited to listen to. In doing this, you can establish credibility surrounding your brand, business, or topic.

That said, if your audience is broader, you should be careful with being overly specific. If you are writing content (especially website content) and are unsure of your audience's specific expertise, you should aim to maintain a simple, conversational tone. No matter who you are writing to, it's important to keep things concise. No one wants to read long sentences. The longer your sentences are, the more likely your readers are to lose sight of your purpose. It's best to keep your sentences short, clear, and to the point. If your sentences are long, try splitting them up to make them more readable.

Chapter 2: Step 2 - Assigning a Purpose to Each Paragraph

When it comes to reading content, no one likes to read large blocks of text. As previously discussed, it is crucial to maintain a sense of clarity and make your reader quickly aware of your purpose. Content writing should be broken up by paragraph, with a clear purpose and position in each. Paragraphs are designed to split the information up into easy-to-swallow sections—each focused on a single, coherent idea.

All sentences in a paragraph should support the main point. In each paragraph you write, you should establish a clear purpose (*why* this paragraph is being written), the tone (*how* you will convey the subject), and the audience (to *who* this paragraph is addressed). One of the best ways to keep yourself on track with this mission is to start a new paragraph with each new idea you introduce and run each paragraph through a "checkpoint" process.

One of the most common mistakes novice writers make is to write disjointed paragraphs that don't seem to have any relation among them. This can be highly confusing for readers. As such, the aim is to link every paragraph so that you transition from one point to another.

A good rule of thumb is to look at each paragraph as an individual point you'd like to make regarding your main idea. As such, it's a type of puzzle that you are putting together as you transition from one part of the discussion to another. Once you put all of the pieces together, you can articulate an argument that makes sense throughout the passage.

So, let's take a look at the most effective tips you can put into practice as you look to write up your content.

Creating Summary Paragraphs

One major way to condense your content and maintain purpose is by creating summary paragraphs. One of the best ways to do this is to write out all of your information, then condense it into the most important pieces. You get practice summarizing every day in your conversations in class, with coworkers, or friends by describing the major highlights, information, and purpose of what you're talking about.

Summary paragraphs work in a very similar way as you condense larger blocks of text into smaller paragraphs using only the most crucial bits of information. It is important to use your own voice as you craft your summary paragraphs, bringing your personal twist to the most important information in your content. Although it is important to keep things brief, you must make sure not to eliminate any key points or pieces of supporting evidence.

Now, it's important to be careful to not include too much information in a single paragraph. Of course, there is a great deal of value in synthesizing your points effectively. The last thing readers want is for you to go on and on when you could have gotten straight to the point. This is very useful in words of non-fiction. As for works of fiction, you need to be sure that you use the right number of words. By "right amount," we mean that you should take your time to describe points as they are intended to be described. For instance, novels require great depth when it comes to describing scenes and characters. Additionally, novels require you to be thorough when presenting a sequence of events. In the case of non-fiction works, you need to present as much information as you can in as few words as possible.

Do you see the difference?

Please keep in mind that this is a skill that can be developed over time. So, please make sure that you take the time to practice your skills so that you can sharpen them as much as possible.

Quickly Answering Reader's Questions

As you write each paragraph, it is crucial to approach the task with your reader in mind. Remember that your reader will likely be reading your content quickly, and you must respond to their needs within that time. Write the most relevant information, and write for your reader to scan the content. Make sure to conduct thorough research to provide relevant information that will answer your reader's questions and meet their needs.

In non-fiction, it is essential to address readers' questions for the get-go. Sure, you might want to take a few words to introduce the topic and build momentum. However, you will lose readers if you take too long to make your point. Readers want you to get straight to the point. After all, they are looking at your content to find value. This value comes in the form of information. This is something they cannot get if your works are filled with fluff. Naturally, getting to the point is crucial. So, try to avoid beating around the bush as much as you can. Address questions directly. Don't hesitate to economize words and lines. The most important thing is to deliver value every step of the way.

Offering Accurate Descriptions

Although it is important to be concise, you must be sure to offer thorough descriptions of your content. As a content writer, it is your job to determine the services and benefits of the content you are writing on. How can you write about the content in your niche in a way that will stick with readers? What benefits set your content apart? Before you begin to write your paragraphs, take time to make a list of the most important points you will be discussing. Play with several ideas for outlines to determine the correct order of events. How can you adequately transition from one paragraph to the next? How can you use your various research points, narrative tools, and statistics to build up to the largest purpose of the content?

Indeed, furnishing accurate descriptions is about stating the right words at the right time. Now, in novels and works of non-fiction, it might be tempting to describe people and places at length. That's fine only if it leads you somewhere. But if you drag things on for too long, you'll eventually lose readers. The idea here is to provide the right level of detail for the topic you're covering.

Consider this situation.

You are working on a technical handbook. This book requires a good level of detail as you need to accurately describe the elements making up the guide. You need to give readers as many details as possible so that they can carry out the task effectively.

Does this mean you need to write extensively on each element?

Not necessarily. What it means is that you need to ensure that your writing is clear enough so that your readers know exactly what you're talking about. Often, that comes with experience. You may not know exactly how much to write in the early going. However, the experience will show you what a reasonable level of detail would be.

A good rule of thumb is to see things from the perspective of your readers. Think about how you would feel if you were reading it. Your descriptions might make perfect sense to you, but they might not make sense to someone else. If anything, you can always ask someone else to take a look at it for you. That way, you can gauge the effectiveness of your writing.

Narrowing Down Main Points

In the case of the election content, you may decide that your main points are as follows: the statistics of college students who vote, the reasons some students feel discouraged from voting, the issues that get students to the polls, and the ultimate results of young people showing up to cast their votes. By dedicating paragraphs to each of these paragraphs you can accurately keep your reader on track and build up to the primary persuasive purpose, which is to get college students to vote.

In this example, you need to be clear about your points. Otherwise, it might be tempting for you to lose sight of your objectives. When you lose sight of your objectives, you tend to rant and wander away from your main points. This can lead to vague passages that don't address your core arguments. This is why sticking to your argument is crucial when it comes to ensuring effective writing. If you feel that a specific sentence or paragraph does not add anything to your core argument, then drop it. Please remember that there is a great deal of value in always sticking to the point. While it might seem restrictive to some degree, the last thing you want is to be overly vague.

Avoiding Passive Sentences

As you write each paragraph, it is important to survey each sentence for passivity. It is crucial to avoid passive sentences at all costs and keep things in the present tense. Content written in the passive voice is not only less engaging but also more clunky and difficult to understand. By keeping your content in the present tense, you can give readers a greater ability to understand the message and be impacted by it. Passive voice is generally employed in academic and scientific texts. So, it's important to keep that in mind as you go through your overall text.

It's also important to keep in mind that using the passive can get tricky. This is especially true if you build long and complex sentences. This is why the passive is generally limited to academic writing. If you're writing fiction, the passive should be avoided as much as possible. This is especially true if you're writing a fast-paced novel. The passive requires a lot more time to process. Therefore, a thriller needs to stay on target as much as possible.

Please bear in mind that the passive is also very impersonal. This is why it is often used in an academic tone. So, if you're looking to create a warm and inviting atmosphere, using the active voice makes the most sense. In doing so, you can keep things personal and close to your audience.

Chapter 3: Step 3 - Determining Main Ideas and Conclusion

We have discussed the importance of breaking the main ideas into paragraphs, but how do you determine the main ideas? In order to determine the main ideas from a longer passage of information, you must be able to execute a critical understanding of the information. One of the first ways to demonstrate this understanding is by reading the passage thoroughly, then identifying the topic. Who or what is this paragraph focused on? In the example with the content directed towards college-aged voters, the *who* is college-aged voters, and the *what* is the election results.

Summarizing Passages

As you seek to develop your main ideas, you must be able to summarize each passage of information. With every testimony, graphic, or piece of research you read to generate your content, you should aim to summarize it in one sentence. How would you describe the main ideas of each of the informational sources you are using in as few words as possible?

Maintaining Overarching Themes

In the search for the main idea, you should pay special attention to the introductory and concluding information. The first and last sentence of your content should make sense in the overall theme of the content, and the main idea should be expressed. In some cases, you may use the first sentence to set a precedent, then use words such as "but", "thus," or "however" to imply that the second sentence is actually where the main idea lies.

Utilizing Repetition

As you write your content, make sure to provide repetition of common ideas. As your reader reads each paragraph, they should be able to easily summarize what it is about. If they are struggling, they will immediately look for repeated words, phrases, and ideas. Therefore, it is crucial to include this repetition as a guide to keep your readers on track. This repetition leaves the reader with no question of what the paragraph is talking about.

Topic and Thesis Sentences

When the main idea is stated directly, it is called the topic sentence. It is useful to include a topic sentence in each paragraph in order to set the precedent for the rest of the paragraph. The topic sentence should provide a clear idea of what the paragraph will discuss, and it should introduce supporting details readers can look to for evidence. If you have several paragraphs on the same topic within your content, you may be better off using an overarching thesis statement, which you can divide into smaller points throughout the piece.

Implying the Main Idea

If you do not define the main idea in direct terms, you still need to imply it. This implied main idea implores readers to examine the content closely, engage deeply with it, and truly understand what you are trying to communicate. They will pay close attention to the word choice, sentence structure, and image you are painting for them, and this will help them to feel more engaged with the content.

Avoiding Main Idea Mistakes

Now you have learned how to determine your main idea and express it in your content, but there are still several crucial mistakes to avoid. Before you define your main idea, you must be sure to use your skills to summarize the main idea of what you want to express in your content. You can do this through intense research on your topic, and seeking conclusive and persuasive evidence. You must avoid being too broad with your main ideas, while still being sure to provide enough information to your readers.

Revisiting Earlier Information

As you move into the conclusion aspect of content writing, it is important to revisit your thesis or topic sentences that were used throughout. You should model your conclusion after your introduction by referring back to the main ideas and information. Re-explain the evidence, testimonies, statistics, etc. that you used to demonstrate the truth in what you said, as well as what you want the reader to do next. Remind the reader of what they have learned, how it will satisfy their needs, and the role they have in engaging with your content. The reader should have no question of what needs to be done next, and they should feel excited to do so.

Avoiding Introductory Phrases

As you begin your conclusion, it is important to avoid phrases like "in conclusion" or "in summary." Phrases like this are cliché and may cause readers to become bored. As odd as it may seem, it is perfectly appropriate to begin a conclusion without a formal introductory phrase. If you do feel the need to introduce it somehow, you should do so by directing readers back to the evidence they have just read with a phrase like "according to the evidence."

Summarizing the Overall Argument

Your conclusion should summarize your main argument in a short 1-2 sentence blurb that compiles all of the main ideas and crucial evidence you provided in your content. Explain how the statistics, testimonials, or research you provided support the mission you are calling your reader to adopt. What are the things that a particular cleaning product apart from the rest? What are the reasons college-aged students should feel inspired to vote? What insider information can readers get from your posts on the real-estate market that they can't get from competing content?

Facing Opposing Arguments

If you have presented a direct argument as a way to prove the superiority of your content, you cannot shy away from opposing arguments. You have to face the opposition head-on, acknowledge it, and prove why it is irrelevant. In the case of the election example, you may say something like "Although many college students feel defeated by the electoral college and feel that their voices do not really matter, statistics show that their votes are crucial to determining election outcomes." This is the perfect Segway into election statistics you can use as supporting evidence.

Leaving a Lasting Impact

As you draw to the end of your conclusion, you must remember that your goal is to leave a lasting impact on the reader. You should end your piece of content writing with a direct call to action and a statement that will stick in your reader's mind. In order to do this, you should make your readers think, feel excited, and feel that their opinions and efforts matter. You must show why this topic matters, and help the reader to feel the same passion as you do. The reader should have no questions about what is expected of them, or what actions they should take in order to meet their own needs or avoid unpleasantries.

You may benefit from using a "fear tactic" of issuing a warning to further motivate readers. Another tactic is to invoke an image, which will help inspire your readers towards a reality that is better than the one they currently live in. You can add to this by predicting how reality may be shaped if your ideas are implemented. If readers can clearly visualize this, they will feel more passionate to act. Additionally, you may use your final sentence to bring up a universal topic that is easy for readers to relate to.

Speaking to All Crucial Points

As you summarize your content in the conclusion, you should be sure to speak to all of the main points. If you do not take the time to revisit every point you made, you may end up weakening the stance of the content and leaving readers with a muddled image in their head. You should make an effort to provide a general overview of the main points, evidence, and calls to action.

Additionally, you must be sure not to introduce any new information in the conclusion. The conclusion should speak to each aspect of your content, nothing more, nothing less. You need to be creative in the language you use and be sure to provide a thorough recap, but you should not add any evidence or information that has not already been said. If you try to add new information, your reader may lose sight of the main points, thus weakening the overall impact of the content. If you come up with new information that you think absolutely must be added, find a place earlier in the content to add it in, as opposed to simply tacking it on to the conclusion.

Chapter 4: Step 4 - Selecting the Correct Language to Use

When it comes to the language you use in a book, it largely depends on your audience. You cannot expect to reach your audience effectively without using the right type of language. Using the right type of language goes beyond the use of correct grammar. This is about using the language to paint the picture that you want your audience to get. Thus, you need to be sure that the language you use hits home.

Selecting the correct language is about understanding the mind of your readers. As such, your choice of language depends on the factors that you want to convey to them as effectively as possible. If you do this correctly, you will get through to your audience effectively. If you don't, then you might find your audience getting confused or missing the point entirely.

Consider this example:

You are writing an academic paper. Naturally, you expect your audience to be educated individuals with college degrees. As such, it would make sense to use a very formal tone and language to present your paper. Now, imagine you did the complete opposite. You used a vibrant and informal tone. That would lead your audience to stop taking you seriously. Using this type of language would lead readers to believe that you are not a serious and credible source.

Can you see how language plays a key role in getting your message across? Please bear in mind that it's not so much what you say, but how you say it. So, let's explore the elements you need to consider when selecting the language you use in your writing.

Writing for Your Audience

The first thing you need to be cognizant of is the audience you're writing for. Knowing them means to understand who they are, where they come from, and why they would read your writing. Also, you need to know how old they are, their level of education, and what they expect to gain from your writing.

At first glance, many of these elements are pretty straightforward. For instance, if you're writing a children's book, you cannot expect to use complicated language. Depending on the age of the child, you would need to use simple language that isn't tough to understand. By the same token, a book for older kids might have a bit more complex language. Still, you would try to keep it as simple as possible.

There are times when you might have to do a little more research. This is generally the case when you write non-fiction material. Non-fiction material needs to be carefully planned. In particular, you need to know more about who your intended readers are. For example, if you're writing a how-to guide, you need to know if these are novice readers or experienced practitioners. Additionally, you might find that some of your readers are not native English speakers. Therefore, understanding complex language might be tough for them. So, you write with these folks in mind.

Knowing your audience is all about tailoring language and content to suit their needs and expectations. Therefore, it's always a good idea to take the time to reflect on who you're writing for. Doing this will save you a ton of headaches down the road.

Know Your Purpose

It is vital that you identify the purpose of your writing. In short, you must be clear about why you are writing in the first place. Ask yourself these questions:

- Am I writing to inform?
- Am I writing to persuade?
- Am I writing to entertain?
- Am I writing to create awareness?
- Am I writing to debate?

Naturally, the answers to these questions will determine the approach you choose to take with your work. For example, if you're writing to entertain, light and playful tone would serve best. Therefore, you would need to use language that reflects this tone.

Knowing your purpose is an important step in delivering the written message. This is critical in creative fiction writing. If you're telling a dramatic tale, then your tone needs to be serious and somber. If this is a horror tale, then you need to be as "creepy" and mysterious as possible. Of course, that would imply using the right type of vocabulary and sentence structure.

In case you are focused more on an academic tone, then it might be best if you considered using more complex structures such as the passive in order to reflect an impartial, third-party tone. Naturally, this requires you to be more careful with the way you articulate your ideas. Otherwise, you might run the risk of confusing folks.

Selecting the Right Vocabulary

The actual vocabulary you use is dependent on your purpose. This is highly important as knowing your purpose will enable you to make sense of what the language you need to use. Consequently, you will make the right choice when it comes to selecting the proper vocabulary.

Let's consider this situation.

You are writing a thriller. In this type of novel, you need a quick, fast-paced tempo that takes the reader through a long sequence of events in a short timeframe. Therefore, you need to be economical with your writing. So, long and drawn-out descriptions won't fly. You need to keep descriptions short and get to the point of events. To achieve this, you would need shorter sentences in which you utilize lots of synonyms. Plus, you would need to ensure you're using simple tenses and clear sentences.

If you're writing an epic novel, readers will not expect a short book. They will expect you to take them on a journey through a fantasy land. Therefore, you need to be as descriptive and explicit as possible. Here, a voluminous use of adjectives is essential to painting the proper picture you want. As such, there is no need to be economical. You can take as much time as you want to set the scene for your reader. While you might still want to keep grammar simple, it is always best to make sure that you don't skimp on the details. When it comes to novels, the devil is in the details.

As you can see, your approach depends on the type of audience, purpose, and message you want to convey. You cannot expect to make a thriller move swiftly by taking the time to stop and smell the roses. By the same token, you can't expect your audience to fully imbibe your epic tale by rushing them through the events.

Selecting the Right Tone

When we talk about "tone," we're talking about the way you choose to say things. In spoken language, the tone is about the inflections in your voice. The tone is also about the speed in which you speak, and the type of accent you place on your words.

In the case of writing, the tone is all about the level of formality you use. Also, tone pertains to the way you frame the information readers get. When you hear about tone, you often see words as "academic," "lively," "serious," and "humorous." All of these words provide an indication of where your book is headed. As such, ensuring that you have the right tone depends on how you want to present your information.

Let's assume you're writing a fiction novel. Your intended audience is young adults aged 18 to 25. Since you know your audience, you know they prefer a light and informal tone. They don't want you to use highly sophisticated words. They want you to keep it simple and to the point. This means that you choose to use commonly used words, short tenses, and mainly in the active voice. You make sure that you don't use long and complex sentences that cause the reader to overly think about their meaning. As such, you want a crisp and fast-moving read. These types of books work well for people on the go.

Now, let's assume that your targeting older readers. So, you're writing a novel that deals with the struggles of life. As such, this is a very mature topic that requires a great deal of reflection and insight. Naturally, you can't expect to have a quick-paced book. You need to take your time to properly present your point, develop your arguments, and state your positions clearly. In the end, you bring about a conclusion that makes sense to the reader. In this example, you can afford to take longer to express your point, while using more complex language and structure. After all, chances are that your readers aren't necessarily on the go. Thus, they can afford to dedicate a little more time to reading.

Ultimately, the tone is about ensuring that you build the proper atmosphere. As such, you can use it to bring the reader into the right state of mind. As you build your argument, you can then drive the point home directly and effectively.

Staying True to Your Personality

One of the hallmarks of all great writers is the ability to let their true personalities shine through. Often, this means using their real voice when writing. Some writers are witty, while others are insightful. Then, you have passionate writers, while others are straight-shooters. The fact is that you need to let your voice shine through your writing. Trying to be something you're not is a sure-fire way of getting stuck. The most prolific writers can produce a great deal of content because they don't hide who they really are.

The first step to letting your personality shine through is to write the way you think. Now, this is easier said than done. It is often difficult to articulate your thoughts in a manner that's comprehensible to others. Yet, it's important to reflect your thought process in your writing.

Consider this example.

Let's suppose you're writing a romance novel. Now, you are not a naturally "romantic" person. Instead, you're more rational and down to Earth. As such, attempting to be poetic is not something that comes naturally to you. So, if you try to be as poetic as you can, you might find it very difficult to get through your novel. In contrast, if you stick to your true self, you'll find that you can put an interesting twist into this novel.

The aim here is to give yourself a chance to be who you are. Don't pretend to be something you're not. Being authentic is about using your words to describe one particular thing. Sure, others will have a different way of describing the same thing. Nevertheless, being able to let your particular voice shine through is essential to creating the right mindset in the reader.

This is what the best writers are capable of.

They transport you to their thought process. In the end, they are able to help you navigate through the maze of thoughts and ideas that lead to the ultimate outcome. Now, readers may not agree with the outcome. However, readers signed up for the trip and not necessarily the outcome. As such, it's your job to take them through a journey they will enjoy every step of the way. You can achieve this by letting your voice shine through. Don't allow yourself to get caught in being "perfect." Unfortunately, that's what a lot of writing classes intend to teach. There is no such thing as perfection. Language is an art that's intended to reflect your individuality. So, make every effort to let that individuality manifest itself.

Chapter 5: Step 5 - Providing Evidence

One of the biggest challenges that writers face is backing up their claims. This is especially important for non-fiction writers. After all, the last thing you want to do is mislead your readers. Providing misleading information is a sure-fire way of getting yourself discredited. Thus, the challenge becomes finding the right ways to back up everything you write.

Providing evidence becomes a question of producing honest and unbiased information. Ideally, you'd be reporting facts. That way, any ideas you share have the proper backup. This will lead you to become a trusted source in your particular area of expertise. Of course, there is no question that we all have our own opinions and biases. In many cases, readers expect you to make your position evident. That is why backing up your work as much as possible is essential to ensuring that you are not just throwing things out there.

As a pro, you need to become aware of the various tools you can use to back up your claims. Mainly, these devices will provide you with the tools you need to position yourself effectively in your area of expertise. So, let's get right down to it.

Why Back Up Your Claims?

There is a difference between fact and opinion. Facts are essential to building a credible argument. Facts provide a solid means of establishing a reasonable foundation for your entire argument. If you fail to do so, your readers might dismiss you altogether. While your writing might be solid, your argument might be flimsy, at best.

So, backing up claims is essential to building a reputation in your chosen area. When you back up everything you write, you instantly vault yourself into another level. This is especially true if you're challenging common beliefs and ideas. Being able to bring forth new ideas with the right sources is a great way of creating content that resonates with readers.

For non-fiction writers, providing facts enables readers to get the right information they need. As you provide them with credible sources, your readers will come to expect the real deal from you. They will come to know that you're not just pulling ideas out of a hat. Your readers will know that you have taken the time to do the research. In the end, the information you provide is filled with valuable information they can rely upon.

As for opinions, please ensure that your opinions are also based on facts. The last thing you want is to put opinions forward that doesn't have any reasonable backing to them. While they may be perfectly logical and consistent, opinions that lack backing gets dismissed or discredited. Ultimately, your opinions won't carry as much weight as well as researched ones. So, it pays to do your homework.

Not All Sources Are Created Equal

It is very important to note that not all sources carry the same weight. Mainly, sources are only as good as their credibility. Therefore, you need to ensure that whomever you cite has the right amount of weight behind them. If you cite sources that don't necessarily have a good reputation, your claims won't be taken seriously.

In the academic world, your sources are vital to ensure you have the right kind of backing. For example, scientific journals, university publications, and peer-reviewed materials are all valid materials to choose from. By the same token, reports from the mainstream media all provide adequate support for your claims, especially when describing events.

In contrast, if you choose sources that don't have adequate backing, then you are risking the validity of your claims. Even if you're assumptions are correct, the sources you cite will discredit your work. As such, you need to make sure you have the sources in mind. For instance, if you cite conspiracy sites as opposed to reputable news agencies, your materials won't have the same level of credibility. By the same token, solid sources may lead you to fine-tune your arguments as they may provide you with ideas and information you hadn't considered. Whenever possible, do a cursory search on academic databases, scientific journals, or mainstream media sources. The better the reputation of your sources, the more credibility your work receives.

Also, quoting subject matter experts is a great way of giving your materials the credibility they need. When you use expert opinions, please make sure that the context fits the overall scheme of your materials. One of the biggest mistakes is to cite an expert only to realize that their opinion somehow contradicts your arguments. Now, if you're using a contradictory opinion for the sake of framing an argument, that's fine. However, please make sure that if you're using expert opinions to support your claims, these had better be in line with what you are trying to achieve.

Types of Sources

Let's take a look at the various types of sources you can use to support your work. Please bear in mind that you want to ensure they come from reputable places and individuals. That way, your work will have the backing it needs to be taken seriously.

Scientific Journals

If your content is academic in nature, then scientific journals make all the sense in the world. You can search for individual journals to see what articles they have published on your chosen topic. Also, you can sift through academic databases. These databases group articles on specific topics published in various journals. That way, you can get a glimpse into the type of literature that's available out there.

Now, there is one caveat to scientific journals. Journals have varying levels of popularity and acceptance. As such, journals are ranked based on their reputation, standing, track record, and quality. So, it's a good idea to do a Google search to find the best-ranked journals in your chosen area. That way, you can start with publications from those journals first, and work your way down. That way, you can be sure that your sources will be taken seriously.

Whenever possible, try to avoid citing studies and papers through the media. For example, you cite a study discussed in a newspaper article. However, it would be much more effective to seek the study itself and use that as your source. The reason for this is that you can get the information you need straight from the source. The last thing you want is to report information that's already been filtered by someone else. After all, you can't be sure that another writer shares the same opinion as you do. Therefore, it makes sense to go straight to the source.

Case Studies

Case studies are a great way to find examples of the point you are attempting to illustrate. Often, case studies provide real-world situations that demonstrate your point. Also, case studies generally show how a theory can be seen in practice. That way, you can show readers how your arguments can be seen in real life.

Another way you can use case studies is to distill key points from them. When you go through one, you can find important lessons, experiences, or concepts that you can use to get your point across. Then readers will use your case study as a means of mirroring their own assumptions. As such, a case study serves to make your point. It is a means of independently verifying what you are looking to prove.

There is one caveat with case studies. Make sure that the circumstance surrounding it is relevant to your audience. For example, if the case study was conducted in a country that's very different from that of your readers, they may have trouble relating to the situation surrounding it. So, please ensure that case studies are as relevant as possible to your readers.

Testimonials

Testimonials can be a bit tricky to use, especially if they don't come from the most credible sources. In particular, testimonials from regular folks work well with advertising. However, if you're looking to back your materials, you might be better off using expert opinions.

When you use a testimonial, you need to be careful about the specific topic you're discussing. For example, if you're talking about a highly scientific topic, then you might be better off sticking to academics and subject matter experts. Now, if you're reporting facts about a specific event, then definitely witness accounts and testimonials from people directly involved are very good places to start.

In the end, testimonials can serve to prove a point, especially when you don't have first-hand knowledge of the situation. First-hand accounts very useful when you're writing a journalistic piece. As for works of fiction, you might be able to incorporate these testimonial accounts within the overall scope of the story. The main point here is to ensure that you maintain credibility. Some authors like to clarify the fact that they are presenting witness accounts and not expert testimony.

On the subject of expert testimony, such accounts from experts during court proceedings, congressional hearings, or sworn statements are all good sources of information. Since these opinions are given under oath, the individuals who furnish them need to be as forthcoming as possible. Unless these expert witnesses flat-out lie, you can be sure that you have a trusted source of information.

News Reports

You need to be careful when it comes to the media. It's important to note that the media doesn't always get it right. Of course, there are trusted publications that have an impeccable reputation. However, that doesn't mean that their work is absolutely perfect. Whenever you use journalistic works are your sources, it's always a good idea to make sure you double-check whatever is stated in their publications. It could be that news reports leave out something important or perhaps miss and key point. As such, you want to make sure you double-check. Otherwise, someone might call you out on your claims. Needless to say, that is something that you want to avoid.

When you look at journalistic works, always try to verify their sources. If you see things such as "a source spoke on a condition of anonymity" then you're dealing with hearsay. While the outlet might be reputable, the information itself cannot be independently verified. Therefore, that opens the door to unnecessary scrutiny. This is why it's always important to verify the information yourself before confidently using it in your material.

Interviews

If you have access to experts and witnesses, you can use interviews as a means of backing up your work. Ideally, you would have full permission from the individual to use their accounts freely. That way, you can use their name as a means of backing up your claims. Most experts are willing to do interviews free of charge. However, you would need to be patient and as transparent as possible.

If you use second-hand interviews, it's always a good idea to contrast the same information from as many sources as possible. Often, media edits interview to fit their airtime or particular agenda. As such, finding unedited versions whenever possible is always a good way of ensuring the quality of the information you present.

Please ensure that you avoid taking interviews out of context. This is rather easy to do, especially when you have a specific bias that you want to pursue. Unless the overall interview fits your narrative, it's always best to be fair. Taking statements out of context can seriously damage your credibility and reputation. Therefore, try your best to use the types of materials that fit your narrative so that you can maintain a consistent narrative throughout your materials.

Chapter 6: Step 6 - Triple-checking Technicalities

Quality is crucial when producing effective materials. In addition to appropriate tone, vocabulary, descriptions, and arguments, you want to ensure that you have the right grammar, spelling, and cohesion. All of these elements are fundamental to producing high-quality content.

Much of this process is done in the editing phase of your content. Editors can help you spot inconsistencies in your arguments, paragraphs, or ideas. Editing is not meant to bash your work. Instead, it's meant to clean it up so that your ideas truly shine through. Otherwise, you could find yourself making needless mistakes.

It's also worth noting that polishing up writing shows readers that you care about them. After all, if you take the time to make sure your work is spic and span, they will feel that you are serious about your work. Naturally, it doesn't matter how good your writing is. If you're sloppy, readers will call you out on it. So, it makes sense to pay attention to detail as much as possible.

So, let's take a look at how you can triple-check the finer points of your writing. In the end, you want to make sure that you put your best foot forward. This will make you seem like the real pro that you are.

Checking Grammar

Grammar is one of the trickiest parts of writing. While there is no question that you can speak the English language appropriately, using proper grammar in writing can lead you to feel out of place at the time. After all, it's one thing to have a conversation, while it's another to write down your ideas clearly and appropriately.

So, checking grammar is crucial to ensuring the right type of material you want others to see. For example, verb tenses can be tricky at times, especially when you're building long, complex sentences. Naturally, it's easier to keep it simple. When you do so, you ensure that you're not making things harder on yourself. In the end, keeping sentences short and clear is always the best way to go.

You ought to be the first line of defense with grammar. You must take the time to ensure that you're using the proper form every time. However, human error is quite possible. It could be that you simply make a mistake. Therefore, the second line of defense is useful. You can enlist grammar-correction software to help you navigate this part. Grammar-correct software uses artificial intelligence to ascertain proper writing. This type of software gets it right most of the time. Of course, it's not perfect. Yet, it can work pretty well on its own.

Lastly, getting an editor to go through your work is highly recommended. Now, you don't need to employ a professional editor or proofreader. Often, a friend or family member can help you spot things you might have missed. As such, it is always a good idea to get another pair of eyes to go through your writing. That way, you can be sure that you're getting things triple-checked effectively.

Ensuring proper vocabulary

By "proper vocabulary," we're not talking about cursing. Instead, we're talking about using the right words you need to get your point across. Many times, the right vocabulary may be technical in nature. In such cases, you might need to get someone specialized to have a look at your content.

There are other times when you might need someone to double-check the way you use specific words. For example, you might use one word or phrase too often. Therefore, having someone else go through your text would reveal such inclinations. In the end, the other person going through your text can help you find other ways of phrasing your ideas.

Proper vocabulary also refers to things use as the use of prepositions, conjunctions, and interjections. These words may be easily corrected by spellcheck software. However, it's worth noting that no software is perfect. Therefore, it's important to have a pair of human eyes to go over your text. This is how you can triple check your efforts.

If you're not confident in software, you can always have two different people go over your text. Sometimes, having two completely different individuals review your text can provide you with a good sense of how well written your text is. The idea is to be as thorough as possible. Being thorough is all about ensuring that the words you are using are being used in the proper context.

Beware of Sounding Smart

A common mistake is attempting to sound smart. This action refers to using words, phrases, and structures that make your writing more intricate than it has to be. Now, there is nothing wrong with using a formal or even academic tone if the situation warrants it. However, it is entirely different when you take a regular text and try to make it sound more complex than it should be. Many times, this is the result of feeling insecure about your writing abilities. Naturally, writers attempt to overcompensate for their perceived lack of originality or talent. However, that could not be farther from the truth. The aim is to let your voice sound true as much as possible.

When you think about your content, it's crucial to write for your audience. Thus, it's critical to avoid trying to impress your audience. When you try to impress others, you get away from your strengths. As such, you won't give yourself the proper opportunity to let your voice manifest itself.

To avoid this situation, try your best to have others judge your writing. The idea of judging is not to "pass" or "fail" your work. The aim is to have others see if your work is a true reflection of who you are. From there, you can feel confident in your ability to make your voice manifest.

Use Beta Testers

The term "beta testing" refers to running real-life trials with a finished product. The aim of a beta test is to determine how real customers react to a specific product. In the end, customer feedback is used to make any final tweaks to the product prior to its final launch.

Beta testing is very common in the software world. However, you can use it for your writing, as well. Conducting this type of testing is quite straightforward. All you need to do is to take your writing and have other folks read it.

That's all.

Then, you offer them the opportunity to critique your work. You can offer them the opportunity to provide you with freeform feedback or a more structured approach such as filling out a worksheet. Either way, your beta testers can offer you insight into the effectiveness of your writing. This feedback can give you a sense of how well you've used vocabulary, terminology, and tone. This type of testing goes beyond the mere act of double-checking grammar and spelling. This is about understanding how well your work resonates with your intended audience.

Please remember that a combination of machine and human intelligence is a great way of polishing up your writing. However, please make sure you don't take things personally. Many times, writers take critique personally. Many times, there is nothing personal. It's just a question of people providing you with an honest take on the impact your writing causes. Ultimately, you always have the opportunity to go back to the drawing board to perfect your work.

Chapter 7: Step 7 - Utilizing Your Passion and Your Voice

Passion is one of the elements that cannot be taught. Passion is all about making your voice manifest throughout your writing. This is the ingredient that great writers are able to make manifest in their work.

When you think of the best writers in history, they are all able to let their true voice shine through regardless of the topic in their writing. For example, great novelists can take seemingly pedestrian events and turn them into great works of literature. Other incredible writers can take run-of-the-mill topics and present them in a lively and entertaining manner.

Making your passion evident is far easier when you actually feel passionate about a topic. But what if you're not really into a topic? What if you're merely writing because you need to? Think of all those school papers you've had to write. How passionate were you about those papers?

Using your voice to manifest your passion is crucial in making your writing stand out above the rest. Your passion is what takes readers on a journey through the various elements needed to go from good to outstanding.

So, let's take a look at how you can use your passion to make your work stand out above the rest.

Make Your Position Clear

When you attempt to make your passion manifest, you must state your position clear. Sometimes, that means taking sides in a debate. Other times, that means staying neutral. The point here is that you want to let your readers know where you stand from the get-go. You can't reasonably expect your readers to take part in your passion if you flip-flop from one position or another.

Let's consider a couple of examples.

First, you're writing an academic work. In this work, you can state your side of the debate. You are forthcoming about your opinions, thereby leading the reader to know what side you're supporting. Also, it could be that your position is to remain neutral, that is, you're not supporting any side in the debate. As such, you present facts, state an argument, and then state conclusions based on your findings. This is a common practice among academics.

Second, you're writing a work of fiction. To make your work that much more personal, you openly take a position as part of your book's narrative. So, you let your narrative reveal what position you have taken. For instance, you're writing a romance novel in which there are clear heroes and villains. Also, you're writing a historical novel in which you seek to expose the wrongdoing of certain individuals in a series of events.

In both cases, you are presenting your position directly to the reader. The difference lies in the way you do it. When writing non-fiction, you can afford to get straight to the point. In fiction writing, you have the luxury of taking the time to get to the point. In either case, the idea is to ensure that you have a clear mindset as you write.

Avoid Becoming a Cheerleader or a Critic

When passion becomes manifest, it can be easy to get carried away. Mainly, you might find yourself singing the praises of a person or events, while you might bash other folks or situations. While we're not advocating that you always remain neutral, it's important for you to state your opinion with a clear and level-headed approach.

Let's consider both sides of the equation.

Firstly, when you favor a specific position, it's vital to state your support and then outline the reasons why you support this position. Then, it's essential to back up your supporting points. Otherwise, you may come off as a cheerleader. Of course, people who agree with your position will be happy to follow along. However, those who do not agree with you might become turned off. Therefore, you want to avoid turning people away. Doing so needlessly risks losing readers.

Secondly, when you oppose a specific position, take the time to explain why you don't favor your position without resorting to needlessly bashing your object of criticism. When you open bash other people and positions, you might come off as bitter or resentful. Needless to say, that is not what you want to portray. If you're clearly opposed to one thing or another, it's essential that you state why you oppose the situation with a clear and consistent argument.

Maintaining a level-headed approach is often hard for professional writers. Allowing your personal bias to remain clearly away from your statements is a must. Therefore, you must ensure that whatever you write, you are always on the same track. Most of all, you need to ensure that your statements and claims are fundamentally true. Otherwise, you risk becoming discredited.

Writing for Fun

For some, writing is a job. For others, writing is a passion, a hobby, a pastime, if you will. For people who truly enjoy writing for the love of it, writing comes a bit more naturally. Writing for fun then becomes an enjoyable task. This is something that often comes through in your words. Unless you write on a topic you hate, your general enthusiasm will peer through your overall work. Readers will be privy to your passion for writing.

This is a rare treat for most readers.

Think about reading the news. Journalists are often detached from the information they report. They merely stick to the facts. Moreover, journalists have templates and formats they follow to ensure they are accurate in their reporting.

Now, compare a run-of-the-mill news report to an editorial. In an editorial, you'll find the writer is truly passionate about the opinions they present. While they may try to remain objective and professional about the position they take, these writers clearly manifest their passion. They do so because they enjoy what they write. To them, writing is an exercise in self-expression.

So, look at writing as a means of expressing your personal individuality. Your readers will come to know the real you from the way you use words to express yourself. Perhaps you might not be the most articulate speaker, but you can definitely use the power of written words to make your readers jump into your psyche.

If you approach writing as a job, please be sure to find a system to help you automate your writing process. There are plenty of courses and systems out there. However, we're going to talk about one approach that's highly successful.

First, begin by briefly introducing your topic. A short background description is enough to give readers a glimpse of what they can expect in the text. This will enable readers to prepare their minds for the upcoming discussion.

Then, state your position. Try to be as clear and objective as possible. Try to avoid using colorful language that makes you a cheerleader or a critic. Also, try to avoid any inflammatory or overly enthusiastic remarks early on.

After, let your readers know that you will present your supporting evidence for your position. Whether it's a work of fiction or non-fiction, you can take the rest of your content to fully develop your argument. As you do so, make sure that you clearly outline your position as logically and consistently as possible. Please try avoiding leapfrogging from one point to another. This will only confuse readers.

Lastly, provide a conclusion in which readers can get a summary of what you have just told them. The practical purpose of this conclusion is to give readers something they can take away with them. From there, you have used a system that you can automate every time you write.

Please keep in mind that writing ought to be an enjoyable process most of the time. If you find it tough to write, don't sweat it. Often, it's a question to find the right time and mindset to produce content. The most important thing is to dedicate time to writing. In the end, you'll be able to produce your very own works much faster than you could have ever imagined.

Conclusion

When you started this guide, you likely had a product or service you were interested in advertising through content writing, and you had the desire to set yourself apart in the content writing industry. You were likely aware of all that is at stake in making your content stand out and motivating your readers, especially in a society that is brimming with new content at every turn.

Throughout the guide, you were provided with the ins and outs of the content writing process, from how to determine your audience, to maintaining engagement, making the main points stand out, introducing and concluding effectively, answering reader's questions, developing clear calls to action, and double-checking technicalities. You learned tactics for remaining consistent and reliable and building a name for yourself through your unique passion and voice.

You learned the benefits of building a community surrounding your content and making readers feel involved and important. and your content by creating a community. You learned how to address common questions and concerns to further develop your credibility and reassure your audience as they engage with the content you write. You became aware of the most common mistakes to avoid, such as being too broad, too narrow, introducing irrelevant information, or forgetting to revisit important points.

You learned how to acknowledge what your readers need, what makes them feel satisfied, and what inspires them to act. Additionally, you learned what kinds of language to use when addressing unique groups, and you developed tactics for keeping readers from getting confused or bored halfway through.

This guide has helped you discover how to capture and maintain reader engagement, as well as how to increase levels of excitement and inspiration in your community of readers. Throughout your content writing journey, this guide is sure to serve as your toolbox to guide your every move.

So, the time has come for you to go out there and show what you're capable of. Indeed, becoming a proficient writer is a question of time and practice. Nevertheless, you have everything you need to get started on your path to perfection. With each passing line and paragraph, you will perfect your craft. Eventually, you will be able to reflect your voice clearly and effectively. Your readers will come to appreciate your contributions.

Ultimately, you will discover that writing is an action that involves joy and satisfaction. Finding your inner voice is crucial to transmitting the message you want people around you to hear. As you develop your own voice, your readers will become attached to your specific brand of writing. This is what differentiates the best writers from the rest of the pack!

More by Jaiden Pemton

Discover all books from the Creative Writing Series by Jaiden Pemton at:

bit.ly/jaiden-pemton

Book 1: *How to Write Fiction*

Book 2: *How to Tell a Story*

Book 3: *How to Write a Screenplay*

Book 4: *How to Write Sales Copy*

Book 5: *How to Edit Writing*

Book 6: *How to Self-Publish*

Book 7: *How to Write Non-Fiction*

Book 8: *How to Write Content*

Themed book bundles available at discounted prices:

bit.ly/jaiden-pemton